2672270

3A

Math in FOCUS®
Singapore Math®
by Marshall Cavendish

Consultant and Author
Dr. Fong Ho Kheong

Authors
Chelvi Ramakrishnan and Michelle Choo

U.S. Consultants
Dr. Richard Bisk
Andy Clark
Patsy F. Kanter

Marshall Cavendish
Education

U.S. Distributor

**Houghton
Mifflin
Harcourt**

© 2015 Marshall Cavendish Education Private Limited

Published by Marshall Cavendish Education
An imprint of Marshall Cavendish Education Private Limited
Times Centre, 1 New Industrial Road, Singapore 536196
Customer Service Hotline: (65) 6213 9444
U.S. Office Tel: (1-914) 332 8888 Fax: (1-914) 332 8882
E-mail: tmesales@mceducation.com
Website: www.mceducation.com

Distributed by
Houghton Mifflin Harcourt
222 Berkeley Street
Boston, MA 02116
Tel: 617-351-5000
Website: www.hmheducation.com/mathinfocus

First published 2015

Math in Focus® Student Book 3A
ISBN 978-0-544-19359-8

Printed in the United States of America

1 2 3 4 5 6 7 8   1401   20 19 18 17 16 15
4500463698   A B C D E

Contents

Numbers to 10,000

Look for **Practice and Problem Solving**

Student Book A and Student Book B	Workbook A and Workbook B
• **Let's Practice!** in every lesson	• **Independent Practice** for every lesson
• Put On Your Thinking Cap! in every chapter	• Put On Your Thinking Cap! in every chapter

Look for **Assessment Opportunities**

Student Book A and Student Book B	Workbook A and Workbook B
• **Quick Check** at the beginning of every chapter to assess chapter readiness • **Guided Learning** after every example or two to assess readiness to continue lesson • **Chapter Review/Test** in every chapter to review or test chapter material	• **Cumulative Reviews** seven times during the year • **Mid-Year and End-of-Year Reviews** to assess test readiness

Mental Math and Estimation

3 Addition up to 10,000

4 Subtraction up to 10,000

5 Using Bar Models: Addition and Subtraction

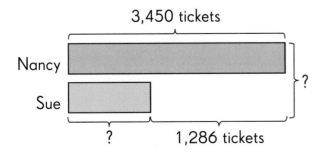

6 Multiplication Tables of 6, 7, 8, and 9

Multiplication

8 Division

Using Bar Models: Multiplication and Division

Welcome to Math in Focus®

This exciting math program comes to you all the way from the country of Singapore. We are sure you will enjoy learning math with the interesting lessons you'll find in these books.

What makes *Math in Focus*® different?

▶ **Two books** You don't write in the ____ in this textbook. This book has a matching **Workbook**. When you see the icon 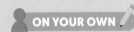, you will write in the **Workbook**.

▶ **Longer lessons** Some lessons may last more than a day, so you can really understand the math.

▶ **Math will make sense** Learn to use bar models to solve word problems with ease.

In this book, look for

Learn
This means you will learn something new.

Guided Learning
Your teacher will help you try some sample problems.

Let's Practice
You practice what you've learned to solve more problems. You can make sure you really understand.

ON YOUR OWN
Now you get to practice with lots of different problems in your own **Workbook**.

Also look forward to *Games, Hands-On Activities, Math Journals, Let's Explore,* and *Put On Your Thinking Cap!*
You will combine logical thinking with math skills and concepts to meet new problem-solving challenges. You will be talking math, thinking math, doing math, and even writing about doing math.

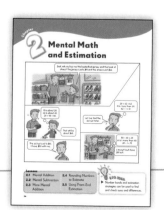

What's in the Workbook?

Math in Focus® will give you time to learn important new concepts and skills and check your understanding. Then you will use the practice pages in the **Workbook** to try:

▶ Solving different problems to practice the new math concept you are learning. In the textbook, keep an eye open for this symbol **ON YOUR OWN**. That will tell you which pages to use for practice.

▶ *Put On Your Thinking Cap!*

    Challenging Practice problems invite you to think in new ways to solve harder problems.

    Problem Solving challenges you to use different strategies to solve problems.

▶ *Math Journal* activities ask you to think about thinking, and then write about that!

Students in Singapore have been using this kind of math program for many years.
Now you can too — are you ready?

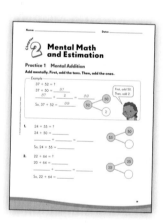

Numbers to 10,000

Mount McKinley
in Alaska: 6,194 m

Pikes Peak
in Colorado: 4,301 m

Mount McKinley is the highest mountain in the United States. It is 6,194 meters high.

Mount Mitchell is the highest peak east of the Mississippi River.

Mount Rainier is higher than Pikes Peak.

Mount Rainier
in Washington: 4,392 m

Mount Mitchell
in North Carolina: 2,037 m

Lessons

1.1 Counting

1.2 Place Value

1.3 Comparing and Ordering
Numbers

BIG IDEA

▶ Count and compare
numbers to 10,000.

Recall Prior Knowledge

Counting on

- Count on by ones: 124   125   126   127   128 ...
- Count on by tens: 134   144   154   164   174 ...
- Count on by hundreds: 124   224   324   424   524 ...

Identifying place value

In 937
- the digit 9 is in the hundreds place.
- the digit 3 is in the tens place.
- the digit 7 is in the ones place.
- Standard form: 937
- Word form: nine hundred thirty-seven
- Expanded form: 900 + 30 + 7

Comparing numbers by using a place-value chart

	Hundreds	Tens	Ones
478	4	7	8
678	6	7	8

Compare the hundreds.
400 is less than 600.
So, 478 is less than 678.

Use < to show *less than*.
So, 478 < 678.

600 is greater than 400.
So, 678 is greater than 478.
Use > to show *greater than*.
So, 678 > 478.

Using place values to order numbers

Order 385, 198, and 627 from least to greatest.

	Hundreds	Tens	Ones
385	3	8	5
198	1	9	8
627	6	2	7

Compare the hundreds.
627 is greater than 385 and 198.
385 is greater than 198.

So, 627 is the greatest, 198 is the least.

Ordered from least to greatest:
198   385   627
least

Counting on and back to find a pattern

Count on by 10 to find the number that is 10 more.

+10   +10

252   262   272   282   292   302   312

Count back by 100 to find the number that is 100 less.

−100   −100

151   251   351   451   551   651   751   851

Count by ones, tens, or hundreds.

1 206 207 208 ⬜ ⬜   **2** 614 714 814 ⬜ ⬜

Express 964 in standard form, word form, and expanded form.

3 standard form ⬜

4 word form ⬜

5 expanded form ⬜

Find the missing number or word.

In the number 327,

6 the digit ⬜ is in the hundreds place.

7 the digit 2 is in the ⬜ place.

Compare the numbers.

8 Which is greater, 99 or 105? ⬜   **9** Which is less, 245 or 708? ⬜

Compare. Write < or > .

10 319 ⬜ 400   **11** 97 ⬜ 164

Find the greatest and least number.
Then order 582, 871, and 339 from greatest to least.

12 ⬜ ⬜ ⬜

Complete each number pattern.

13 842 852 862 ⬜ 882 ⬜

14 671 571 471 ⬜ ⬜ 171

1.1 Counting

Lesson Objectives

- Use base-ten blocks to count, read, and write numbers to 10,000.
- Count by 1s, 10s, 100s, and 1,000s to 10,000.

Vocabulary
word form
standard form

Learn Use base-ten blocks to show numbers.

How many 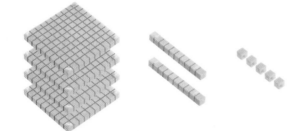 are there?

There are four hundred twenty-five .

There are 425 .

Put ten in a stack.

| 100 | 200 | 300 | 400 | 500 |
| 600 | 700 | 800 | 900 | 1,000 |

1,000

one thousand

10 hundreds = 1,000

Learn

Express a number in different forms.

How many  are there?

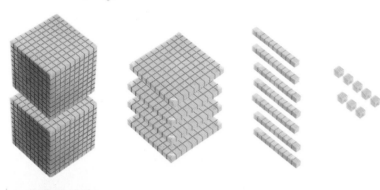

Word form: two thousand, four hundred seventy-eight
Standard form: 2,478

Guided Learning

Look at the base-ten blocks. How many  are there?

1 Express in word form.

2 Express in standard form.

Express in word form.

3 6,257

4 8,540

5 7,601

6 3,094

Express in standard form.

7 eight thousand, six hundred twenty-nine

8 four thousand, seven hundred thirty

9 five thousand, eighty-four

10 seven thousand, ten

Learn

Count to ten thousand.

What number comes after 9,999?

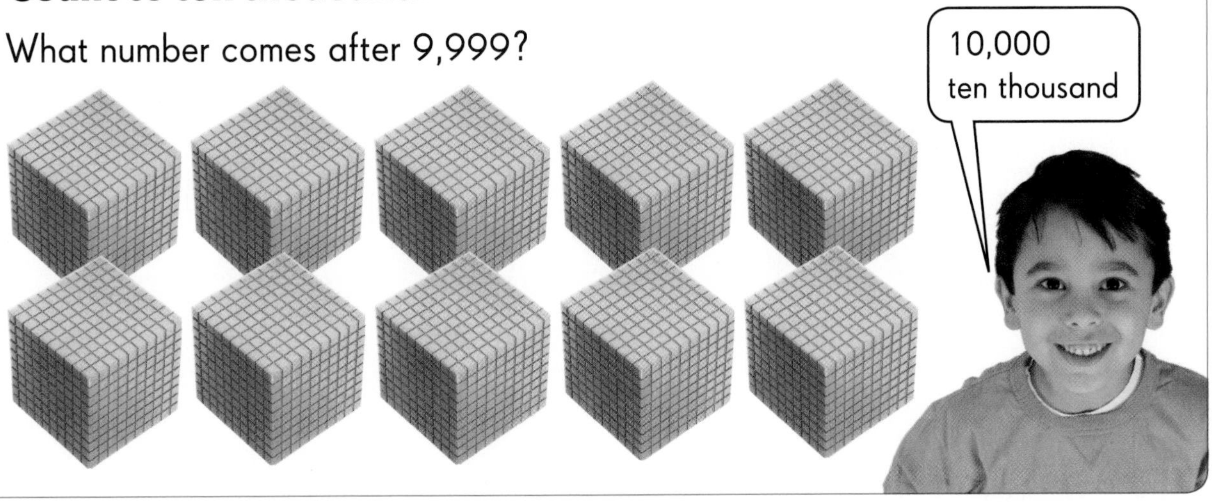
10,000
ten thousand

Learn

Count on by ones.

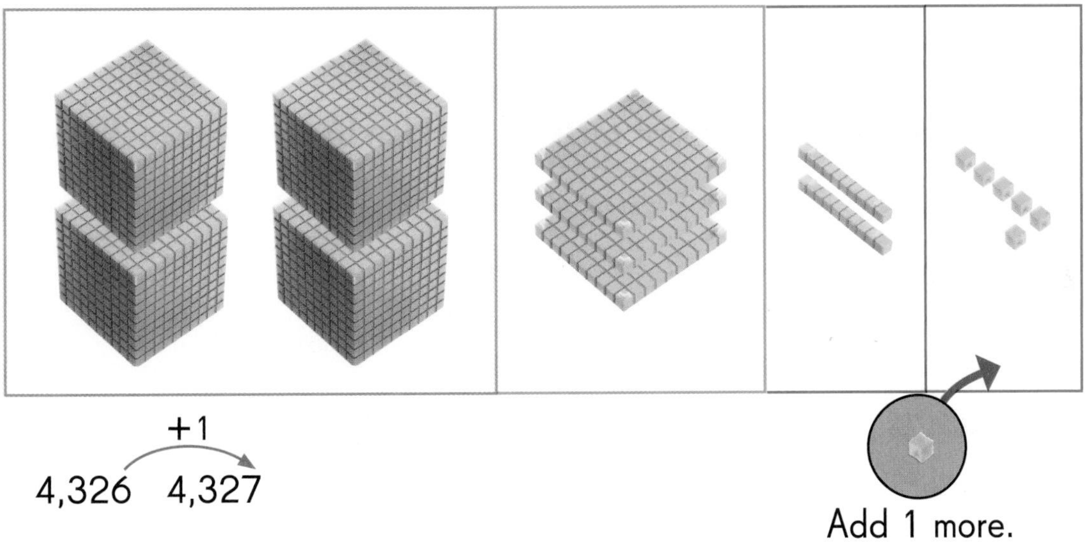
+1
4,326 4,327
Add 1 more.

Guided Learning

**Find each missing number. Count on by ones.
Use base-ten blocks to help you.**

11. 1,342 1,343 1,344 ___ ___ ___
12. 7,085 7,086 7,087 ___ ___ ___
13. 3,497 3,498 3,499 ___ ___ ___
14. 9,994 9,995 9,996 ___ ___ ___

Count on by tens.

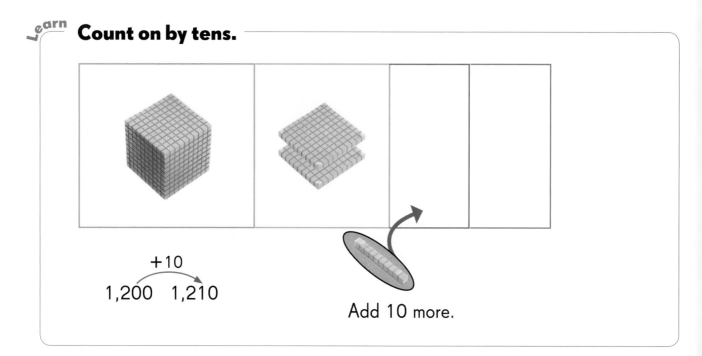

+10

1,200   1,210

Add 10 more.

Guided Learning

Find each missing number. Count on by tens. Use base-ten blocks to help you.

15 3,840   3,850   3,860

16 6,161   6,171   6,181

Count on by hundreds.

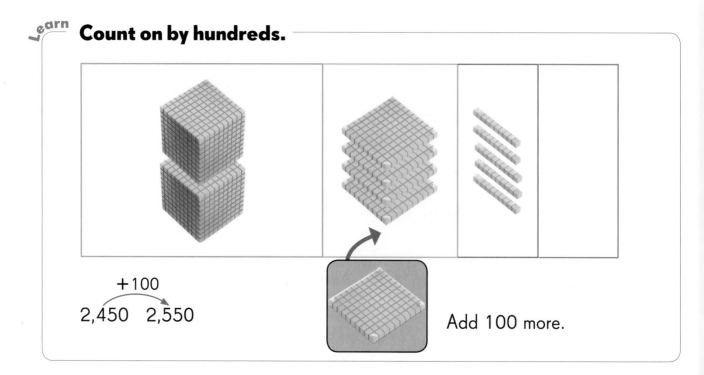

+100

2,450   2,550

Add 100 more.

Guided Learning

Find each missing number. Count on by hundreds.
Use base-ten blocks to help you.

17 5,345 5,445 5,545 ▢ ▢ ▢

18 8,670 8,770 8,870 ▢ ▢ ▢

Learn **Count on by thousands.**

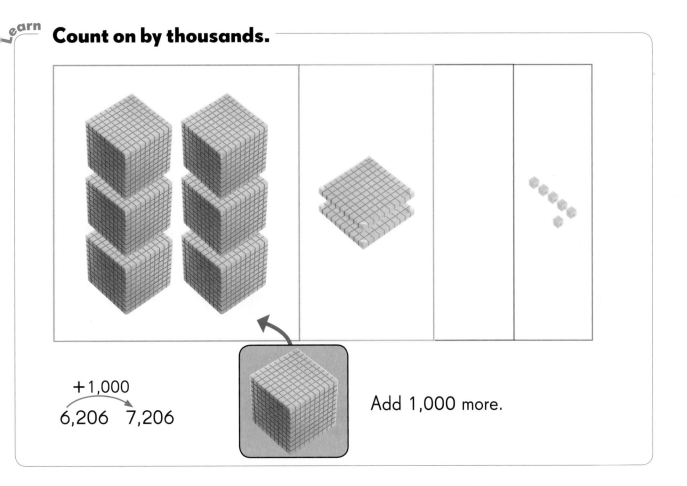

+1,000
6,206 7,206

Add 1,000 more.

Guided Learning

Find each missing number. Count on by thousands.
Use base-ten blocks to help you.

19 4,792 5,792 6,792 ▢ ▢ ▢

20 287 1,287 2,287 ▢ ▢ ▢

21 90 1,090 2,090 ▢ ▢ ▢

Let's Practice

Look at the base-ten blocks.
Express each number in standard form and word form.

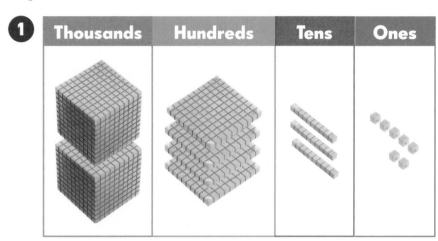

Standard form:

Word form:

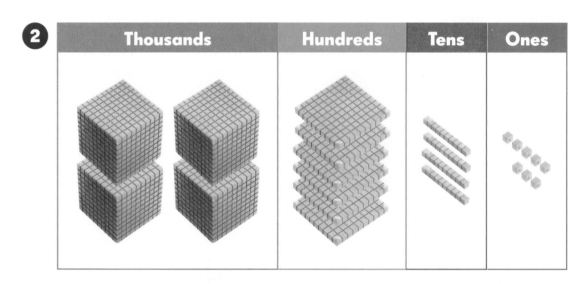

Standard form:

Word form:

Look at the base-ten blocks. Express each number in standard form.

3

Thousands	Hundreds	Tens	Ones

The chart shows the number _____.

4

Thousands	Hundreds	Tens	Ones

The chart shows the number _____.

Find each missing number.
Count on by ones, tens, hundreds, or thousands.

5 1,427 1,428 1,429 ____ ____ ____

6 4,356 4,366 4,376 ____ ____ ____

7 7,608 7,708 7,808 ____ ____ ____

8 90 1,090 2,090 ____ ____ ____

ON YOUR OWN

Go to Workbook A:
Practice 1, pages 1–4

1.2 Place Value

Lesson Objectives

- Use base-ten blocks and a place-value chart to read, write, and represent numbers to 10,000.

- Read and write numbers to 10,000 in standard form, expanded form, and word form.

Vocabulary
digit
place-value chart
value
place-value strips
expanded form

Learn **Use a place-value chart and place-value strips to find the value of each digit in a number.**

How many  are there?

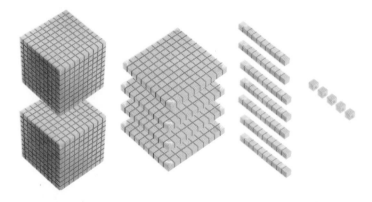

Thousands	Hundreds	Tens	Ones
2	4	7	5

stands for	stands for	stands for	stands for
2 thousands or 2,000	4 hundreds or 400	7 tens or 70	5 ones or 5

This is a **place-value chart**.

In 2,475,
the **digit** 2 is in the thousands place.
the digit 2 stands for 2 thousands or 2,000.
the **value** of the digit 2 is 2,000.

These are **place-value strips**.

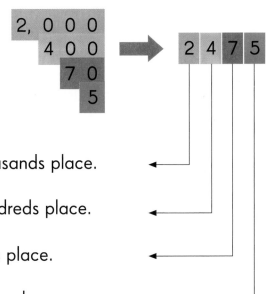

The digit 2 is in the thousands place.

The digit 4 is in the hundreds place.

The digit 7 is in the tens place.

The digit 5 is in the ones place.

2,000, 400, 70, and 5 make 2,475.

The word form of 2,475 is two thousand, four hundred seventy-five.

2,475 = 2 thousands, 4 hundreds 7 tens 5 ones
      = 2,000 + 400 + 70 + 5

2,000 + 400 + 70 + 5 is the **expanded form** of 2,475.

Guided Learning

How many are there? Find the missing numbers.

Thousands	Hundreds	Tens	Ones

1 1,329 = [   ] thousand [   ] hundreds [   ] tens [   ] ones

2 1,329 = [   ] + [   ] + [   ] + [   ]

3 In 1,329,

the digit [   ] is in the thousands place.

it stands for [   ].

its value is [   ].

Find each missing number or word. Use base-ten blocks to help you.

4 In 2,548,

the digit [   ] is in the hundreds place.

the digit 4 stands for [   ].

the value of the digit 8 is [   ].

5 In 2,562, the values of the digit 2 are:

2, 5 6 2

[   ] ←┘   └→ [   ]

Read the place-value strips and complete each sentence.

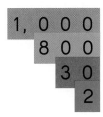

1,000, 800, 30, and 2 make 1,832.

6 ⬜ is the standard form of 1,832.

7 ⬜ is the word form of 1,832.

8 ⬜ is the expanded form of 1,832.

7,000 and 5 make 7,005.

9 ⬜ is the standard form of 7,005.

10 ⬜ is the word form of 7,005.

11 ⬜ is the expanded form of 7,005.

Roll and Show!

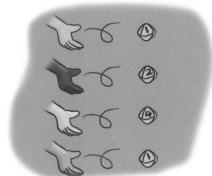

Players: **4 to 8**
Materials:
- one 10-sided die
- base-ten blocks
- place-value chart

STEP 1 Form two groups, the Rollies and the Showies.

STEP 2 The Rollies roll the die four times to get four numerals.

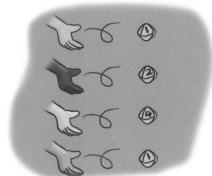

STEP 3 The Showies use these numerals to make a 4-digit number. Then they write the number in a place-value chart and show the number using base-ten blocks.

STEP 4 Each group takes turns to roll and show.

The group with the most correct answers wins!

Use a place-value chart and base-ten blocks to show greater numbers.

I have 4,827.

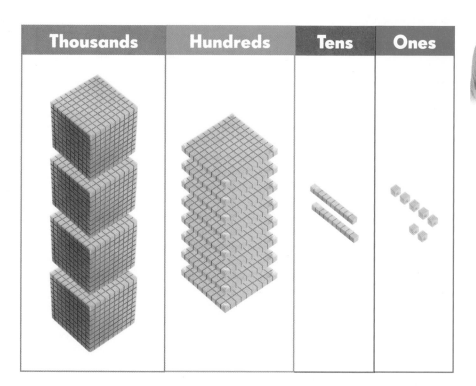

Thousands	Hundreds	Tens	Ones

4,000
800
20
7

4 thousands 8 hundreds 2 tens 7 ones = 4,827

4,000 + 800 + 20 + 7 = 4,827

4,000, 800, 20, and 7 make 4,827.

Guided Learning

Find each missing number. Use base-ten blocks to help you.

12 5,000, 300, 10, and 6 make [ ] .

13 7,000, 200, 80, and 9 make [ ] .

14 3,000 + 100 + 70 + 5 = [ ] .

Find each missing word or number.

15 What is the value of each digit?

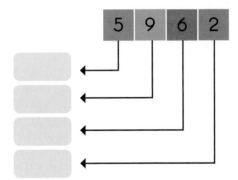

16 In 6,925,

the digit [ ] is in the thousands place.

the digit 9 stands for [ ] .

the value of the digit 2 is [ ] .

Find each missing number.

17 [ ] , 300, 60, and 1 make 4,361.

18 6,720 is 6,000, 700, and [ ] .

Find each missing number.

19 3,000 + 900 + 10 + 5 = [ ]

20 1,324 = [ ] + 300 + 20 + 4

Let's Practice

Find each missing number.

1

Thousands	Hundreds	Tens	Ones
3	7	0	0

[ ] thousands   [ ] hundreds   [ ] tens   [ ] ones

The number is [ ].

Express the number formed with the place-value strips in standard form, word form, and expanded form.

```
4, 0 0 0
     8 0 0
       6 0
         5
```

2 standard form [ ]

3 word form [ ]

4 expanded form [ ]

Find each missing number.

5 In 2,839 the digit [ ] is in the thousands place.

6 In 3,571 the digit 5 stands for [ ].

7 In 6,042 the value of the digit 4 is [ ].

Find each missing number.

8 5,000, [ ], and 5 make 5,805.

9 7,610 = 7,000 + [ ] + 10

10 4,000 + 50 = [ ]

11 8 + 500 + 9,000 = [ ]

ON YOUR OWN

**Go to Workbook A:
Practice 2, pages 5–10**

1.3 Comparing and Ordering Numbers

Lesson Objectives

- Use base-ten blocks to compare and order numbers.

- Use place value to compare and order numbers.

Vocabulary

greater than (>)	greatest
less than (<)	rule
least	number line

Learn Use base-ten blocks to compare and order numbers.

Which is greater, 4,051 or 3,785?

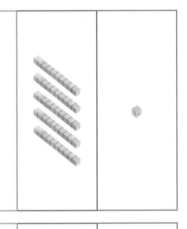

4,051

3,785

Compare the thousands.
4,051 is greater than 3,785.
4,051 > 3,785

4 thousands is **greater than** 3 thousands.

Guided Learning

Compare the numbers. Choose > or <.

1

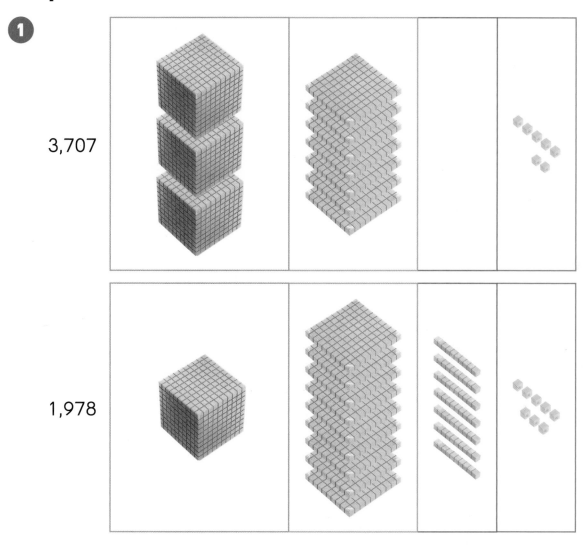

3,707

1,978

3,707 is ⬤ 1,978.

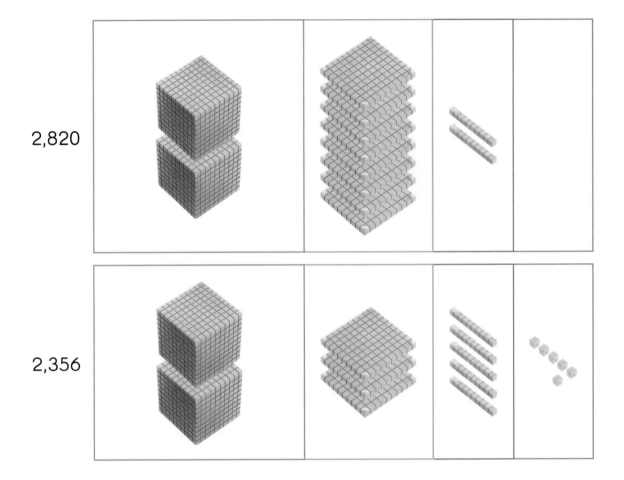 Use base-ten blocks to compare and order numbers.

Which is less, 2,820 or 2,356?

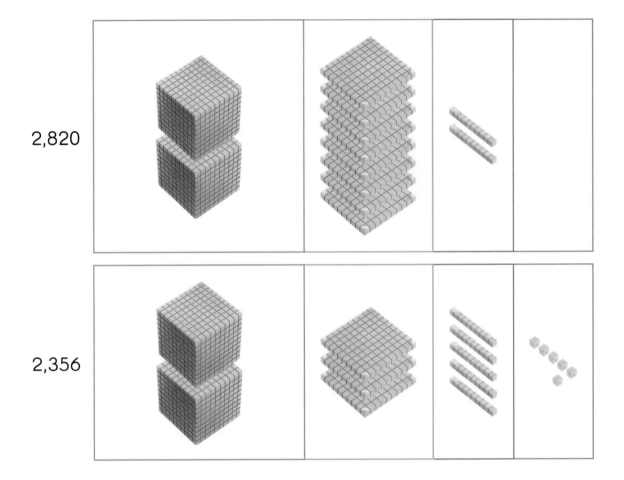

2,820

2,356

Step 1 Compare the thousands. They are the same.
Step 2 Compare the hundreds.

3 hundreds is **less than** 8 hundreds.

2,356 is less than 2,820.
2,356 < 2,820

> The two numbers may have the same number of thousands.
> Then you should compare the hundreds.

22   **Chapter 1**   Numbers to 10,000

Guided Learning

Compare the numbers. Choose > or <.

2

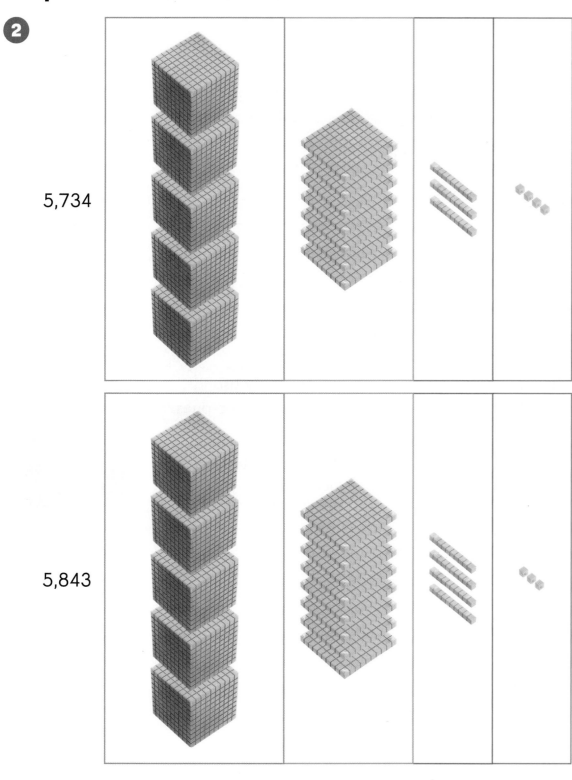

5,734

5,843

5,734 is ⬤ 5,843.

^earn Use place values to compare numbers.

Compare 6,829 and 6,870.

Which is greater?
Which is less?

> The two numbers may have the same number of thousands and hundreds. Then you should compare the tens.

6,870 is greater than 6,829.

6,829 is less than 6,870.

> 2 tens is less than 7 tens.

Compare 2,748 and 2,745.

Which is greater?

> The two numbers have the same number of thousands, hundreds, and tens. Then you should compare the ones.

2,748 is greater than 2,745.

2,748 > 2,745

> 8 ones is greater than than 5 ones.

Guided Learning

Compare. Write < or >.

3 4,058 is ◯ 4,610.

4 6,289 is ◯ 6,280.

Using place values to order numbers.

Order 2,389,   3,001, and 3,010 from least to greatest.

	Thousands	Hundreds	Tens	Ones
2,389	2	3	8	9
3,001	3	0	0	1
3,010	3	0	1	0

Compare the thousands.

3,010 and 3,001 are greater than 2,389.
3,010 and 3,001 have the same number of thousands and hundreds.

You should compare the tens.
3,010 is greater than 3,001.

So, 3,010 is the **greatest** .

2,389 is the **least** .

Ordered from least to greatest:

2,389   3,001   3,010
 least

Guided Learning

Compare 4,769, 4,802, and 4,738.

5 Which is the least?

Which is the greatest?

Order the numbers from greatest to least.

6 4,790 974 7,049 9,107

Hands-On Activity

Players: 2
Materials:
• worksheet

STEP **1**

2,314

Player 1 thinks of a 4-digit number with 1, 2, 3, and 4.
Use each digit only once.

STEP **2** Player 2 writes his or her first guess in the first row of the worksheet.

Thousands	Hundreds	Tens	Ones
1	2	4	3

STEP **3**

Player 1 gives some clues.
For example, if Player 1's number is 2,314 and Player 2's guess is 1,243, Player 1 says:
• My thousands is greater than yours.
• My hundreds is greater than yours.
• My tens is less than yours.
• My ones is greater than yours.

STEP **4** Player 2 writes his or her second guess in the second row.
If his or her guess is 2,134
Player 1 will say:
• My thousands is the same as yours.
• My hundreds is greater than yours.
• My tens is less than yours.
• My ones is the same as yours.

Thousands	Hundreds	Tens	Ones
1	2	4	3
2	1	3	4

STEP **5**

Thousands	Hundreds	Tens	Ones
1	2	4	3
②	1	3	④

Player 2 circles the numbers that are the same as Player 1's.
Player 2 goes on guessing until he or she gets the correct number.
Switch roles and play again!

Look for patterns on a number line.

Some numbers on the **number line** are missing.
Find the missing numbers.

> To find the missing number, look for a pattern. Its **rule** is to add 10 to the number before it.
>
> + 10
> 1,457   1,467

10 more than
1,457 is 1,467.

1,427 1,437 1,447 1,457 ? 1,477 1,487 ? 1,507 1,517 1,527

10 less than
1,507 is 1,497.

> To find the missing number, the rule for the pattern can also be to subtract 10 from the number after it.
>
> − 10
> 1,497   1,507

Guided Learning

Look for a pattern. Find each missing number.

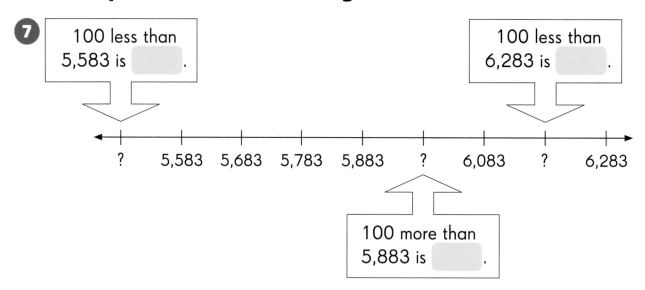

7 100 less than 5,583 is [ ].

100 less than 6,283 is [ ].

100 more than 5,883 is [ ].

? 5,583 5,683 5,783 5,883 ? 6,083 ? 6,283

Find each missing number. Use a number line to help you.

8 10 more than 5,893 is [ ].

9 100 less than 3,967 is [ ].

Look for a pattern. Find each missing number.

10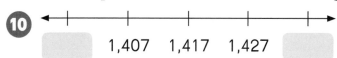

[ ] 1,407 1,417 1,427 [ ]

Complete each number pattern. Use a number line to help you.

11 5,843 5,833 [ ] 5,813 [ ] [ ]

12 [ ] [ ] 6,913 [ ] 6,933 6,943

13 7,662 [ ] 7,862 7,962 [ ] [ ]

14 4,420 4,320 [ ] 4,120 4,020 [ ]

Let's Practice

Compare. Write < or >.

1 999 ⬤ 8,950

2 2,800 ⬤ 2,080

Find each missing number.

3 10 less than 3,415 is [   ] .

4 100 more than 4,237 is [   ] .

Look for a pattern. Find each missing number.

5

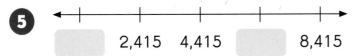

[   ] 2,415 4,415 [   ] 8,415

6

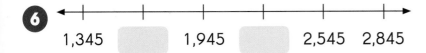

1,345 [   ] 1,945 [   ] 2,545 2,845

Complete each number pattern. Use a number line to help you.

7 7,200 7,220 7,240 [   ] 7,280 [   ] 7,320

8 880 980 [   ] [   ] 1,280 1,380 1,480 [   ] 1,680

9 8,472 8,672 [   ] [   ] 9,272 9,472 9,672

ON YOUR OWN

**Go to Workbook A:
Practice 3, pages 11–16**

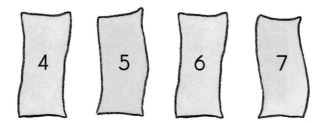

Use these cards. Make as many numbers as possible with:

1 4 in the thousands place

2 6 in the thousands place

3 How many numbers are there in all?

Subtract the least number from the greatest number in the set of numbers with:

4 4 in the thousands place

5 6 in the thousands place

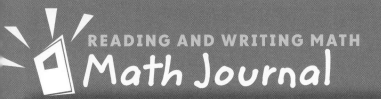
List the steps to arrange the numbers in order from least to greatest.

Example

1,984   2,084   1,884

STEP 1 I compare the thousands.

STEP 2 I can see that 2,084 is the greatest.

STEP 3 I compare the hundreds.

STEP 4 I can see that 1,884 is the least number.

Arranged from least to greatest:

1,884   1,984   2,084
 least

9,049   9,654   8,785

Arranged from least to greatest:

⬚   ⬚   ⬚

List the steps to get your answer.

PROBLEM SOLVING

Rita wrote three 4-digit numbers on a sheet of paper.
She accidentally spilled some ink on the paper.
Some digits were covered by the ink.
Using the clues given, help Rita find the digits covered by the ink.

CLUES

The sum of all the ones is 17.

The ones digit of the first number is the greatest 1-digit number.

The digit in the tens place of the second number is one more than the digit in the tens place of the first number.

The tens digit of the third number is 4 less than the tens digit of the second number.

ON YOUR OWN

**Go to Workbook A:
Put On Your Thinking Cap!
pages 17–18**

Chapter Wrap Up

Study Guide

You have learned...

Numbers to 10,000

Read, Write, and Count

9,745
- Expanded form:
  9,000 + 700 + 40 + 5
- Word form:
  nine thousand, seven hundred forty-five
- Standard form: 9,745

Count by
- ones: 3,928   3,929   3,930...
- tens : 2,096   2,106   2,116...
- hundreds: 813   913   1,013...
- thousands: 4,126   5,126   6,126...

Compare and Order

| 1,638 | 1,728 | 1,629 | 2,268 |

Order the numbers from greatest to least.

- Compare the thousands.
  2,268 is the greatest number.
- Compare the hundreds.
  1,728 is greater than 1,638 and 1,629.
- Compare the tens.
  1,629 is the least number.
  2,268   1,728   1,638   1,629
  greatest

Place Value

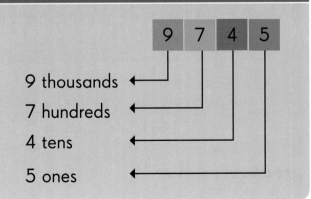

| 9 | 7 | 4 | 5 |

9 thousands ◄

7 hundreds ◄

4 tens ◄

5 ones ◄

Patterns

Number Patterns   +10
- 2,304   2,314   2,324   2,334...
               +100
- 3,619   3,719   3,819   3,919...
               −10
- 5, 811   5,801   5,791   5,781...
               −100
- 7,235   7,135   7,035   6,935...

Chapter Review/Test

Vocabulary
Choose the correct word.

1 The ___ form of 3,614 is 3,000 + 600 + 10 + 4.

2 In a 4-digit whole number, the greatest place value is ___.

3 The ___ form of 2,193 is 2,193.

Concepts and Skills
Express each number in different forms.

4 Express 8,056 in word form. ___

5 Express 6,254 in standard form and expanded form. ___

Complete.

In 1,984,

6 the digit 9 is in the ___ place.

7 the value of the digit 1 is ___.

8 the digit 8 stands for ___.

Compare. Write > or <.

9 3,765 ___ 3,657

10 6,212 ___ 8,523

Identify the least number and the greatest number.

11 3,615   3,156   3,561

Order the numbers from least to greatest.

12 6,028 8,620 960   _960 6028 8620_

13 9,143 9,034 9,134   _9,034 9,134 9,143_

14 3,256 3,279 3,238   _3,238 3,256 3,279_

15 7,425 7,429 7,420   _7,420 7,425 7,429_

Find each missing number.

16 1 more than 6,722 is _6,723_.

17 10 more than 2,863 is _2,873_.

18 100 more than 829 is _929_.

19 1,000 more than 988 is ____.

20 1 less than 3,890 is ____.

21 10 less than 8,742 is ____.

22 100 less than 526 is ____.

23 1,000 less than 4,059 is ____.

Complete each number pattern.

24 3,645 3,545 3,445 ____ 3,245

25 5,014 6,014 ____ 8,014 9,014

Mental Math and Estimation

BIG IDEA

▶ Number bonds and estimation strategies can be used to find and check sums and differences.

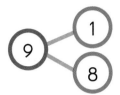

Recall Prior Knowledge

Making number bonds

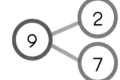

Adding using number bonds

4 + 5 = 9

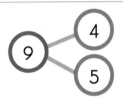

Adding by making 10

7 + 5 = ?

7 + 3 = 10

10 + 2 = 12

So, 7 + 5 = 12.

Addition using the 'adding 10, then subtracting the extra ones' strategy

24 + 7 = ?

24 + 10 = 34

34 − 3 = 31

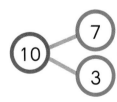

So, 24 + 7 = 31.

Adding 7 is the same as adding 10, then subtracting 3.

Subtracting using number bonds

$8 - 3 = 5$

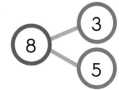

Subtraction using the 'subtracting 10, then adding the extra ones' strategy

$35 - 8 = ?$

$35 - 10 = 25$

$25 + 2 = 27$

So, $35 - 8 = 27$.

Subtracting 8 is the same as subtracting 10, then adding 2.

Rounding to estimate sums and differences and to check reasonableness of answers

$249 + 42 = 291$	$374 - 58 = 316$
249 is about 250.	374 is about 370.
42 is about 40.	58 is about 60.
$250 + 40 = 290$	$370 - 60 = 310$
$249 + 42$ is about 290.	$374 - 58$ is about 310.
The answer is reasonable.	The answer is reasonable.

Find the missing numbers.

 ① ⑦ — 5

 ② ⑦ — 3

Find the missing numbers.

③ 6 = [ ] + 5

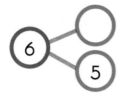

④ 2 + [ ] = 10

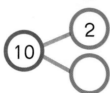

Add by making 10.

⑤ Find 6 + 9.

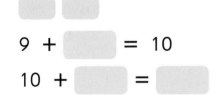

9 + [ ] = 10

10 + [ ] = [ ]

So, 6 + 9 = [ ].

Add. Use the 'adding 10, then subtracting the extra ones' strategy.

⑥ Find 26 + 8.

26 + [ ] = [ ]

[ ] − [ ] = [ ]

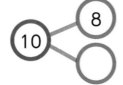

So, 26 + 8 = [ ].

Find the missing numbers.

7 9 − 3 = [ ]

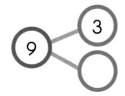

8 5 − [ ] = 1

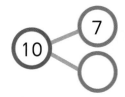

Subtract. Use the 'subtracting 10, then adding the extra ones' strategy.

9 Find 55 − 7.

55 − [ ] = [ ]

[ ] + [ ] = [ ]

So, 55 − 7 = [ ] .

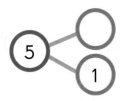

Solve.

10 Find the sum of 319 and 73. Use rounding to check that your answer is reasonable. [ ]

11 Find the difference between 825 and 98. Use rounding to check that your answer is reasonable. [ ]

Lesson Objective

* Add 2-digit numbers mentally with or without regrouping.

Learn **Add 2-digit numbers mentally using the 'add the tens, then add the ones' strategy.**

Find 34 + 52.

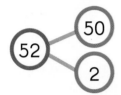

52 = 5 tens 2 ones

Step 1 Add 5 tens to 34.   34 + 50 = 84

Step 2 Add 2 ones to the result.   84 + 2 = 86

So, 34 + 52 = 86.

Guided Learning

Add mentally. Use number bonds to help you.

1 Find 45 + 23.

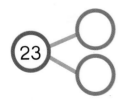

23 = [ ] tens [ ] ones

Step 1 Add [ ] tens to 45.   45 + [ ] = [ ]

Step 2 Add [ ] ones to the result.   [ ] + [ ] = [ ]

So, 45 + 23 = [ ].

Add 2-digit numbers mentally using the 'add the tens, then subtract the extra ones' strategy.

Find 34 + 48.

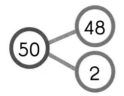

Step 1 Add 50 to 34.   34 + 50 = 84

Step 2 Subtract 2 from the result.   84 − 2 = 82

So, 34 + 48 = 82.

> Do you know why you add 50 and then subtract 2?

Guided Learning

Add mentally. Use number bonds to help you.

2 Find 35 + 57.

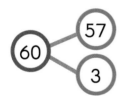

Step 1 Add [   ] to 35.   35 + [   ] = [   ]

Step 2 Subtract [   ] from the result.   [   ] − [   ] = [   ]

So, 35 + 57 = [   ].

Add Mentally!

Players: **2 to 5**
Material:
- cards with numbers from 35 to 55

STEP **1** Player 1 says a number from 11 to 44.

STEP **2** Player 1 then draws a card.

STEP **3** Player 1 adds the two numbers mentally and tells the other players his or her answer.

20 + 46 = 66

STEP **4** The other players check the answer. Player 1 gets 1 point if the answer is correct.

STEP **5** Return the card to the table and mix them up. Take turns to play three rounds each.

The player with the most points wins!

Let's Practice

Find the missing numbers.

1 38 = 3 tens [ ] ones

2 62 = [ ] tens 2 ones

Add mentally. Use number bonds to help you.

3 Find 11 + 37.

37 = [ ] + [ ]

11 + [ ] = [ ]

[ ] + [ ] = [ ]

So, 11 + 37 = [ ].

4 Find 66 + 23.

23 = [ ] + [ ]

66 + [ ] = [ ]

[ ] + [ ] = [ ]

So, 66 + 23 = [ ].

5 25 + 42 = [ ]

6 56 + 32 = [ ]

7 33 + 46 = [ ]

8 41 + 57 = [ ]

Add mentally. Use number bonds to help you.

9 Find 46 + 47.

46 + 50 = [ ]

[ ] − 3 = [ ]

So, 46 + 47 = [ ].

10 Find 28 + 36.

28 + 40 = [ ]

[ ] − 4 = [ ]

So, 28 + 36 = [ ].

11 13 + 49 = [ ]

12 24 + 48 = [ ]

13 37 + 56 = [ ]

14 56 + 28 = [ ]

ON YOUR OWN

Go to Workbook A:
Practice 1, pages 19–20

Mental Subtraction

Lesson Objective

- Subtract 2-digit numbers mentally with or without regrouping.

Learn **Subtract 2-digit numbers mentally using the 'subtract the tens, then subtract the ones' strategy.**

Find 87 − 34.

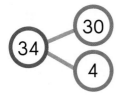

34 = 3 tens 4 ones

Step 1 Subtract 3 tens from 87.   87 − 30 = 57

Step 2 Subtract 4 ones from the result.   57 − 4 = 53

So, 87 − 34 = 53.

Guided Learning

Subtract mentally. Use number bonds to help you.

1 Find 79 − 45.

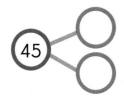

45 = [　] tens [　] ones

Step 1 Subtract [　] tens from 79.   79 − [　] = [　]

Step 2 Subtract [　] ones from the result.   [　] − [　] = [　]

So, 79 − 45 = [　].

Subtract 2-digit numbers mentally using the 'subtract the tens, then add the extra ones' strategy.

Find 63 — 48.

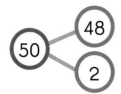

Step 1 Subtract 50 from 63.   63 — 50 = 13

Step 2 Add 2 to the result.   13 + 2 = 15

So, 63 — 48 = 15.

Do you know why you subtract 50 and then add 2?

Guided Learning

Subtract mentally. Use number bonds to help you.

2 Find 72 — 47.

Step 1 Subtract [ ] from 72.   72 — [ ] = [ ]

Step 2 Add [ ] to the result.   [ ] + [ ] = [ ]

So, 72 — 47 = [ ].

3 96 — 38 = [ ]

Subtract Mentally!

Players: **2 to 5**
Materials:
• cards with numbers from 35 to 55

STEP 1 Player 1 says a number from 11 to 99.

80

STEP 2 Player 1 then draws a card.

35

STEP 3 Player 1 mentally subtracts the number that is less from the greater number, and gives the other players his or her answer.

80 − 35 = 45

STEP 4 The other players check the answer. Player 1 gets 1 point if the answer is correct.

45 + 35 = 80
35 + ___ = 80

STEP 5 Return the card to the table and mix the cards up. Take turns to play three rounds each.

The player with the most points wins!

Let's Practice

Find the missing numbers.

1 $42 = 40 +$ ▭

2 $76 =$ ▭ $+ 6$

Subtract mentally. Use number bonds to help you.

3 Find $77 - 46$.

$46 =$ ▭ $+$ ▭

$77 -$ ▭ $=$ ▭

▭ $-$ ▭ $=$ ▭

So, $77 - 46 =$ ▭ .

4 Find $66 - 23$.

$23 =$ ▭ $+$ ▭

$66 -$ ▭ $=$ ▭

▭ $-$ ▭ $=$ ▭

So, $66 - 23 =$ ▭ .

5 $49 - 26 =$ ▭

6 $76 - 42 =$ ▭

7 $87 - 34 =$ ▭

8 $98 - 23 =$ ▭

Subtract mentally. Use number bonds to help you.

9 Find $65 - 47$.

$65 - 50 =$ ▭

▭ $+$ ▭ $=$ ▭

So, $65 - 47 =$ ▭ .

10 Find $73 - 46$.

$73 - 50 =$ ▭

▭ $+$ ▭ $=$ ▭

So, $73 - 46 =$ ▭ .

11 $64 - 38 =$ ▭

12 $72 - 46 =$ ▭

13 $82 - 67 =$ ▭

14 $95 - 29 =$ ▭

ON YOUR OWN

Go to Workbook A:
Practice 2, pages 21–24

 **More Mental Addition**

Lesson Objective

• Use different strategies to add 2-digit numbers close to 100 mentally.

Learn **Add 2-digit numbers mentally using the 'adding 100, then subtracting the extra ones' strategy.**

Find 86 + 95.

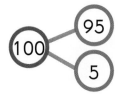

Step 1 Add 100 to 86.   86 + 100 = 186

Step 2 Subtract 5 from 186. 186 − 5 = 181

So, 86 + 95 = 181.

Do you know why you add 100 and then subtract 5?

Guided Learning

Add mentally. Use number bonds to help you.

1 Find 75 + 98.

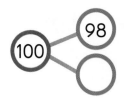

Step 1 Add 100 to 75.   [ ] + [ ] = [ ]

Step 2 Subtract [ ] from [ ].   [ ] − [ ] = [ ]

So, 75 + 98 = [ ].

Add 2-digit numbers mentally using the 'add the hundreds, then subtract the extra ones' strategy.

Find 94 + 97.

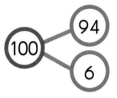 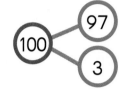 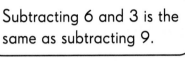

94 and 97 are each near 100.

Step 1 Add the hundreds.
100 + 100 = 200

Subtracting 6 and 3 is the same as subtracting 9.

Step 2 Subtract 6 and 3 from 200.
200 − 6 − 3 = 191

So, 94 + 97 = 191.

Guided Learning

Add mentally. Use number bonds to help you.

2 Find 95 + 99.

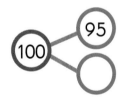 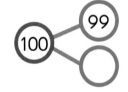

95 and 99 are each near 100.

Step 1 Add the hundreds.

100 + 100 = ⬜

Step 2 Subtract the ones from ⬜ .

⬜ − ⬜ − ⬜ = ⬜

So, 95 + 99 = ⬜ .

More Mental Addition!

Players: **2 to 5**
Materials:
• a number cube
• cards with numbers 92 to 99

 STEP 1 Player 1 rolls the number cube twice to make a 2-digit number.

 STEP 2 Player 1 then draws a card.

STEP 3 Player 1 mentally adds the two numbers and tells the other players his or her answer.

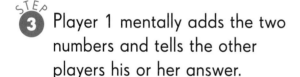

65 + 99 = 164

STEP 4 The other players check the answer. Player 1 gets 1 point if the answer is correct.

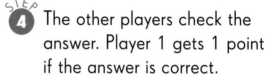

164 − 99 = 65

+65 = 164

 STEP 5 Return the card to the table and mix the cards up. Take turns to play three rounds each.

The player with the most points wins!

Let's Practice

Add mentally. Use number bonds to help you.

1 Find 63 + 99.

63 + 100 = ▢

▢ – ▢ = ▢

So, 63 + 99 = ▢.

2 Find 47 + 97.

47 + 100 = ▢

▢ – ▢ = ▢

So, 47 + 97 = ▢.

3 28 + 99 = ▢

4 38 + 96 = ▢

5 48 + 95 = ▢

6 41 + 98 = ▢

Add mentally. Use number bonds to help you.

7 92 + 96 = ▢

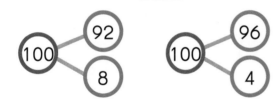

8 98 + 95 = ▢

9 93 + 99 = ▢

ON YOUR OWN

**Go to Workbook A:
Practice 3, page 25–26**

Rounding Numbers to Estimate

Lesson Objective

- Round numbers to estimate sums and differences.

Vocabulary
rounded
estimate
reasonable

Round a 3-digit number down to the nearest hundred.

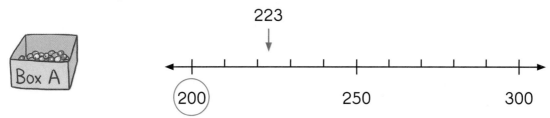

223 beads are in Box A. The number of beads in Box A is 200 when rounded to the nearest hundred.

223 is between 200 and 300. It is nearer to 200 than to 300 on the number line. So, 223 is 200 when **rounded** to the nearest hundred. 223 is about 200.

200 is an **estimate**. It is a number that is close to the exact number.

Round a 3-digit number up to the nearest hundred.

287 beads are in Box B. The number of beads in Box B is 300 when rounded to the nearest hundred.

287 is between 200 and 300. It is nearer to 300 than to 200 on the number line. So, 287 is 300 when rounded to the nearest hundred. 287 is about 300.

Continued on next page

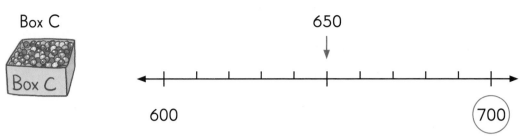

Box C

650

600   700

650 beads are in Box C.
The number of beads in Box C
is 700 when rounded to the
nearest hundred.

650 is exactly halfway between 600
and 700 on the number line.
So, 650 is 700 when rounded to the
nearest hundred.
650 is about 700.

Rounding to the nearest 100. Look at the digit in the tens place.
If it is 1, 2, 3, or 4, round to the hundred that is less. If it is 5, 6, 7, 8,
or 9, round to the greater hundred.

Guided Learning

Round each number to the nearest hundred.

1 216

2 550

3 360

4 950

ᴸᵉᵃʳⁿ Round a 4-digit number to the nearest hundred.

Round 2,329 and 2,382 to the nearest hundred.

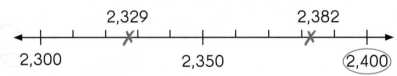

2,329   2,382

2,300   2,350   2,400

2,329 is between 2,300 and 2,400.
It is nearer to 2,300 than to 2,400
on the number line.
So, 2,329 is 2,300 when rounded
to the nearest hundred.
2,329 is about 2,300.

2,382 is between 2,300 and 2,400.
It is nearer to 2,400 than to 2,300
on the number line.
So, 2,382 is 2,400 when rounded
to the nearest hundred.
2,382 is about 2,400.

Guided Learning

Round 4,632 to the nearest hundred.

⑤

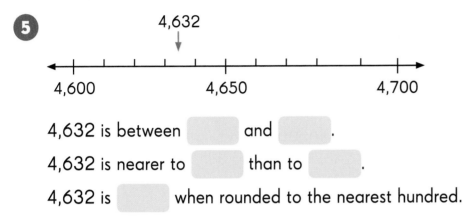

4,632 is between ⬚ and ⬚ .

4,632 is nearer to ⬚ than to ⬚ .

4,632 is ⬚ when rounded to the nearest hundred.

For each number, draw a number line and mark (X) the number on the number line.
Use the number line to round each number to the nearest hundred and circle it.

> ### Example
>
> Round 8,950 to the nearest hundred.
>
> To decide on where to start and end a number line, look at each number and find the nearest hundred before and after it. In the example, 8,950 is between these two nearest hundreds.
>
> 8,900 ←nearest hundred before it 8,950 nearest hundred after it→ 9,000
>
> So, the number line for 8,950 starts at 8,900 and ends at 9,000.
>
>
>
> 8,950 is 9,000 when rounded to the nearest hundred.

⑥ 5,050 ⬚

⑦ 4,158 ⬚

⑧ 2,502 ⬚

⑨ 9,050 ⬚

Round each number to the nearest ten and hundred.

Number	Rounded to the Nearest	
	Ten	Hundred
10 68		
11 482		
12 3,209		

Use number lines to help you.

13 List five whole numbers that round to 2,800 when rounded to the nearest hundred.

Use your answers to mark (**X**) the least and the greatest numbers on the number line.

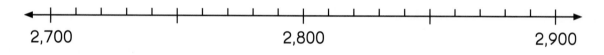

2,700   2,800   2,900

Mark (*X*) the least and the greatest numbers on the number line that round to 9,300 when rounded to the nearest hundred.

14

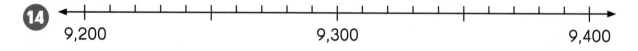

9,200   9,300   9,400

Hands-On Activity

Look at the map below. It shows the driving distances between some U.S. cities and Kansas City.

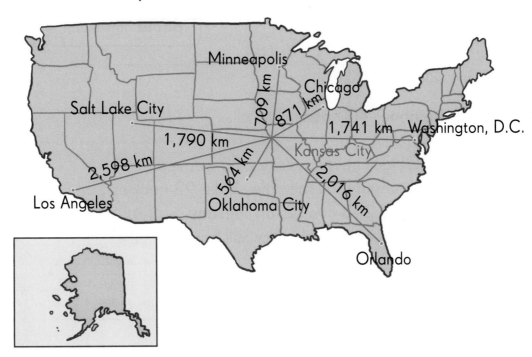

Round each distance to the nearest hundred kilometers.

Example

The distance between Kansas City and Minneapolis is 709 kilometers. 709 kilometers is 700 kilometers when rounded to the nearest hundred kilometers.

Decide whether to find an estimate or an exact amount.

Nita has 178 pennies in her piggy bank.
Eduardo has 231 pennies in his piggy bank.
About how many pennies do they have in all?

Round the number of pennies
each child has to the nearest hundred.

You can estimate
the answer since
the question asks
'about how many'.

178 rounds to 200.
231 rounds to 200.

200 + 200 = 400

They have about 400 pennies in all.

. . . .

Some Girl Guides have to make 500 oatmeal
cookies for a charity fun fair. They bake 92 cookies
on Monday and 268 cookies on Tuesday.
How many more cookies do they still have to make?

92 + 268 = 360
500 − 360 = 140

An exact answer is needed since the
question asks 'how many more'.

They still have to make 140 more cookies.

Guided Learning

Decide whether to find an estimate or an exact answer. Solve.

15 Mrs. Thornton is 59 inches tall.
She wears heels that are 3 inches tall.
How tall is Mrs. Thornton with her shoes on?

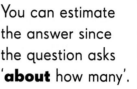

59 in.   ? in.

3 in.

16 A bakery sells 379 muffins on Monday.
It sells 481 muffins on Tuesday.
About how many muffins does it sell on both days?

Decide whether to find an estimate or an exact amount.

Mrs. Blake has $900. She wants to buy an oven for $257
and a washing machine for $518.
Does Mrs. Blake have enough money?

Do you need an
exact answer or an
estimate?

You can use an estimate to see if
Mrs. Blake has enough money.

Round each amount of money to the nearest hundred.
257 is 300.
518 is 500.
300 + 500 = 800
Mrs. Blake has enough money.

· ·

Darren has $379.

After buying two of the chairs, Darren has $136 left.

a How much do the two chairs cost?

b Which two chairs does Darren buy?

SALE
Dining chair $105
Arm chair $177
Computer chair $138

Do you need
an exact
answer or an
estimate?

a You need an exact answer since the
question asks **'how much'**.
$379 − $136 = $243
The two chairs cost $243.

b An estimate is enough to decide which two chairs Darren buys.
Round the cost of each item to the nearest hundred.
Dining chair   105 rounds to 100.
Arm chair   177 rounds to 200.
Computer chair   138 rounds to 100.

$243 is closer to
$200 than $300.

$100 + $200 = $300
The dining chair and the arm chair cost about $300.
$100 + $100 = $200
The dining chair and the computer chair cost about $200.
So, Darren buys the dining chair and the computer chair.

Guided Learning

Decide whether to find an estimate or an exact answer. Solve.

17 A tennis club orders 715 tennis balls
After some matches, 318 balls are worn out.
The remaining matches will use 415 tennis balls.
Does the club have enough balls for the remaining matches?

18 Maria has 557 beads. She gives 156 beads to her sister.
She wants to use the rest of the beads to make two patterns in her dress.
Pattern A   159 beads
Pattern B   301 beads
Pattern C   242 beads

a How many beads does she use to make the patterns?

b Which two patterns can she sew?

19 Renaldo wants to tile his floor.
He has 899 tiles.
172 tiles are damaged.
Bedroom   235 tiles
Living room   489 tiles
Kitchen room   656 tiles

a How many tiles does he have left to tile his floors?

b Which two rooms can he tile?

Learn · Use rounding to check the reasonableness of sums.

Find 182 + 415.

Then use rounding to check that your answer is reasonable.

182 + 415 = 597

Step 1 Round each number to the nearest hundred.

182 rounds to 200.

415 rounds to 400.

> 182 is about 200.
> 415 is about 400.

Step 2 Add the rounded numbers.

200 + 400 = 600

So, 182 + 415 is about 600.

597 is close to 600, so the answer is **reasonable**.

Guided Learning

Find the sum. Then use rounding to check that your answer is reasonable.

20 Find 281 + 532.

281 + 532 = [   ]

281 rounded to the nearest hundred is [   ].

532 rounded to the nearest hundred is [   ].

[   ] + [   ] = [   ]

So, 281 + 532 is about [   ].

Is your answer reasonable? [   ]

Find the sum. Then use rounding to check that your answer is reasonable. Round each number to the nearest hundred.

21 434 + 512 = [   ]
Is your answer reasonable? [   ]

22 818 + 103 = [   ]
Is your answer reasonable? [   ]

Learn Use rounding to check the reasonableness of differences.

Find 588 − 275.

Then use rounding to check that your answer is reasonable.

588 − 275 = 313

Step 1 Round each number to the nearest hundred.

588 rounds to 600.

275 rounds to 300.

588 is about 600.
275 is about 300.

Step 2 Subtract the rounded numbers.

600 − 300 = 300

So, 588 − 275 is about 300.

313 is close to 300, so the answer is reasonable.

Guided Learning

Find the difference. Then use rounding to check that your answer is reasonable. Round each given number to the nearest hundred.

23 Find 677 − 311.

677 − 311 = [ ]

677 rounded to the nearest hundred is [ ].

311 rounded to the nearest hundred is [ ].

[ ] − [ ] = [ ]

So, 677 − 311 is about [ ].

Is your answer reasonable? [ ]

24 426 − 296 = [ ]

Is your answer reasonable? [ ]

25 852 − 463 = [ ]

Is your answer reasonable? [ ]

Let's Practice

Mark (X) each number on the number line.
Then round each number to the nearest hundred and circle it on the number line.

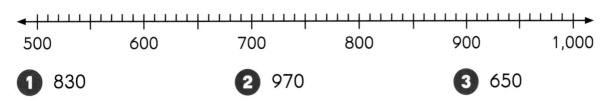

500   600   700   800   900   1,000

1 830   **2** 970   **3** 650

Draw a number line and mark (X) each number on the number line. Then, round the number to the nearest hundred and circle it on the number line.

4 4,283   **5** 3,267   **6** 7,235

Find the sum or difference. Then use rounding to check that your answer is reasonable.

7 501 + 286 ▢   **8** 478 − 214 ▢

9 368 + 495 ▢   **10** 827 − 459 ▢

Solve. Find the estimate.

11 Mrs. Smith wants to buy a pair of pants that costs $168 and a handbag which costs $535. Estimate the total cost of the two items. Would Mrs. Smith have enough money to buy the two items if she had $600? ▢

12 Tanya has $158 and the cost of a bookshelf is $317. About how much more does she need to buy the bookshelf? ▢

ON YOUR OWN

Go to Workbook A:
Practice 4, page 27–30

Lesson 2.5 Using Front-End Estimation

Lesson Objective
- Use front-end estimation to estimate sums and differences.

Vocabulary
leading digit
front-end estimation

Learn Find the leading digit in a number.

Look at the numbers.

438   **2**,875

The front-end or leading digit for **4**38 is 4.

The front-end or leading digit for **2**,875 is 2.

The **leading digit** in a number is the digit with the greatest place value.

Guided Learning

Name the leading digit in each number.

1 712

2 567

3 309

4 9,543

5 2,485

6 8,021

Complete.

7 Write a 3-digit number where the leading digit is 9.

8 Write a 3-digit number where the leading digit is 5.

9 Write a 4-digit number where the leading digit is 3.

10 Write a 4-digit number where the leading digit is 8.

Use front-end estimation to estimate sums and differences.

Estimate 609 + 395.

609 + 395

↓ ↓

600 + 300 = 900

The leading digit of **6**09 is 6.
The leading digit of **3**95 is 3.

. . . .

Estimate 764 − 385.

764 − 385

↓ ↓

700 − 300 = 400

764 **3**85

↑ ↑

Leading digits

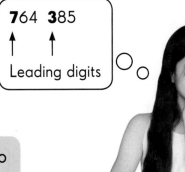

Front-end estimation uses leading digits to estimate sums and differences.

Guided Learning

Solve.
Use front-end estimation to help you.

11 Mr. Moore buys 329 paper clips.
Mrs. Moore buys 518 paper clips
Estimate the number of paper clips they have in all.

12 Brendan collects 987 bookmarks.
Casey collects 475 bookmarks.
About how many more bookmarks does Brendan have than Casey?

Use front-end estimation to check reasonableness of sums and differences.

Find 636 + 289.

636 + 289 = 925

636 + 289

↓ ↓

600 + 200 = 800

The estimated sum is 800.

So, the answer is reasonable.

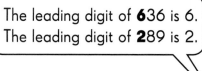

The leading digit of **6**36 is 6.
The leading digit of **2**89 is 2.

Find 514 − 135.

514 − 135 = 379

514 − 135

↓ ↓

500 − 100 = 400

The estimated difference is 400.

So, the answer is reasonable.

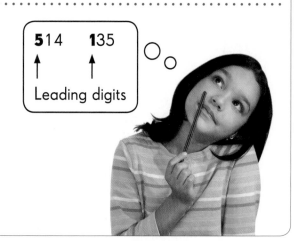

514   **1**35

↑   ↑

Leading digits

Guided Learning

Find the sum. Then use front-end estimation to check that your answer is reasonable.

13 Find 520 + 479.

520 + 479 = [ ]

527 + 479

↓ ↓

[ ] + [ ] = [ ]

The estimated sum is [ ].

Is your answer reasonable? [ ]

Find the difference. Then use front-end estimation to check that your answer is reasonable.

14 Find $715 - 586$.

$715 - 586 = \boxed{}$

$715 \quad - \quad 586$

$\downarrow \qquad\qquad \downarrow$

$\boxed{} - \boxed{} = \boxed{}$

The estimated difference is $\boxed{}$. Is your answer reasonable? $\boxed{}$

Solve. Check that your answer is reasonable.

15 Jolene walks 472 meters.

Ronald walks 394 meters.

Find the total distance they walk.

$472 + 394 = \boxed{}$

$472 \quad + \quad 394$

$\downarrow \qquad\qquad \downarrow$

$\boxed{} + \boxed{} = \boxed{}$

The estimated distance is $\boxed{}$. Is your answer reasonable? $\boxed{}$

16 Mr. Morris sells 726 oranges on a day.

Mrs. Morris sells 654 oranges on the same day.

How many more oranges does Mr. Morris sell?

$726 - 654 = \boxed{}$

$726 \quad - \quad 654$

$\downarrow \qquad\qquad \downarrow$

$\boxed{} - \boxed{} = \boxed{}$

The estimated difference is $\boxed{}$. Is your answer reasonable? $\boxed{}$

Let's Practice

Name the leading digit in each number.

1 487 [ ]

2 354 [ ]

3 5,762 [ ]

4 6,735 [ ]

5 8,649 [ ]

6 9,582 [ ]

Find each sum. Then use front-end estimation to check that your answer is reasonable.

7 354 + 187 = [ ]

8 742 + 254 = [ ]

9 665 + 168 = [ ]

Find each difference. Then use front-end estimation to check that your answer is reasonable.

10 673 − 154 = [ ]

11 574 − 487 = [ ]

12 739 − 572 = [ ]

Solve. Use front-end estimation to estimate.

13 Jennifer has $228. She needs $654 more to buy a television set. Estimate the cost of the television set. [ ]

14 In January, Mr. Estrada's water bill is $47.
In February, his water bill increased to $89.
Estimate how much more his water bill for February is. [ ]

ON YOUR OWN

**Go to Workbook A:
Practice 5, pages 31–34**

Look at the estimates.
Decide if you agree. Explain your answer.

1 683 + 568 is about 600 + 600.

So, 683 + 568 is about 1,200.

Explanation:

2 510 − 257 is about 500 − 200.

So, 510 − 257 is about 300.

Explanation:

CRITICAL THINKING SKILLS
Put On Your Thinking Cap!

PROBLEM SOLVING

Jean has two 3-digit numbers.

She uses front-end estimation to estimate the sum of the two numbers. Her estimated answer is 800.

Find 3 possible sets of two numbers that are not more than 500 each.

Show your work.

ON YOUR OWN

Go to Workbook A:
Put On Your Thinking Cap!
pages 37–38

Chapter Wrap Up

Study Guide
You have learned...

Mental Addition

Add the tens, then add the ones.
Find $36 + 41$.

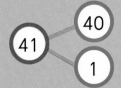

$36 + 40 = 76$

$76 + 1 = 77$

So, $36 + 41 = 77$.

Add the tens, then subtract the extra ones.
Find $36 + 46$.

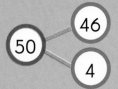

$36 + 50 = 86$

$86 - 4 = 82$

So, $36 + 46 = 82$.

Mental Subtraction

Subtract the tens, then subtract the ones.
Find $55 - 23$.

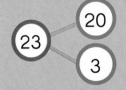

$55 - 20 = 35$

$35 - 3 = 32$

So, $55 - 23 = 32$.

Subtract the tens, then add the extra ones.
Find $72 - 37$.

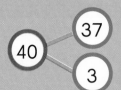

$72 - 40 = 32$

$32 + 3 = 35$

So, $72 - 37 = 35$.

More Mental Addition

Add 100, then subtract the extra ones.
Find $39 + 96$.

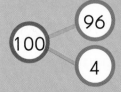

$39 + 100 = 139$

$139 - 4 = 135$

So, $39 + 96 = 135$.

Add the hundreds, then subtract the extra ones.
Find $97 + 98$.

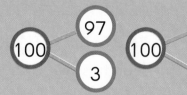

$100 + 100 = 200$

$200 - 3 - 2 = 195$

So, $97 + 98 = 195$.

▶ Number bonds and estimation strategies can be used to find and check sums and differences.

Estimation

To estimate
- the sum of two numbers using rounding or front-end estimation
- the difference between two numbers using rounding or front-end estimation.

To use the estimated sums or differences to check that exact answers are reasonable.

Rounded to nearest hundred	Front-end estimation
Round to the nearest hundred, then add or subtract. Find 365 + 519.	Use the value of the leading digits to add or subtract. Find 365 + 519
365 + 519 = 884	365 + 519 = 884
365 rounds to 400. 519 rounds to 500. 400 + 500 = 900	365 + 519 ↓ ↓ 300 + 500 = 800
884 is about 900. So, the answer is reasonable.	884 is about 800. So, the answer is reasonable.
Find 769 − 314.	Find 769 − 314
769 − 314 = 455	769 − 314 = 455
769 rounds to 800. 314 rounds to 300. 800 − 300 = 500	769 − 314 ↓ ↓ 700 − 300 = 400
455 is about 500. So, the answer is reasonable.	455 is about 400. So, the answer is reasonable.

Chapter Review/Test

Vocabulary
Choose the correct word.

1 677 is about 700 when   to the nearest hundred.

2 The   in a number is the digit with the greatest place value.

3   uses the leading digit to estimate a sum or a difference.

Concepts and Skills
Add mentally.

4 27 + 62 =

5 47 + 86 =

6 39 + 96 =

7 98 + 95 =

Subtract mentally.

8 87 − 62 =

9 65 − 27 =

10 53 − 11 =

11 98 − 44 =

Find each sum or difference. Then use rounding to check that your answer is reasonable.

12) 215 + 143 =

13) 564 + 994 =

14) 615 − 323 =

15) 864 − 702 =

Find each sum or difference. Then use front-end estimation to check that your answer is reasonable.

16) 632 + 421 =

17) 636 − 519 =

Problem Solving

Solve. Find the estimate.

18) Paul has 72 cards. He gives away 59 cards. About how many cards does he have left?

19) Rick has $99. He saves another $46. Estimate the amount of money he has now.

20) The Drama Club has $416 to spend on the next play. Costumes cost $185. Make up costs $176. Estimate the total cost of costumes and make-up. Estimate the amount of money left after buying the two items.

3 Addition up to 10,000

Knock! Knock!
Who's there?
One more.
One more who?
One more to add to 99.
And now we have 100!

Knock! Knock!
Who's there?
One more.
One more who?
One more to add to 999.
And now we have 1,000!

Knock! Knock!
Who's there?
One more.
One more who?
One more to add to 9,999.
And now we have 10,000!

Lessons

3.1 Addition Without Regrouping

3.2 Addition with Regrouping in Hundreds

3.3 Addition with Regrouping in Ones, Tens, and Hundreds

BIG IDEA

▶ Greater numbers can be added the same way 2-digit numbers are added, with or without regrouping.

Recall Prior Knowledge

Finding the sum

45 + 23 = ?

```
    4 5
  + 2 3
  ─────
    6 8  ← sum
```

The sum of 45 and 23 is 68.

Adding 3-digit numbers without regrouping

452 + 235 = ?

Step 1 Add the ones.
```
    4 5 2
  + 2 3 5
  ───────
        7
```

Step 2 Add the tens.
```
    4 5 2
  + 2 3 5
  ───────
      8 7
```

Step 3 Add the hundreds.
```
    4 5 2
  + 2 3 5
  ───────
    6 8 7
```

Adding 3-digit numbers with regrouping

243 + 178 = ?

Step 1 Add the ones.
Regroup the ones.
```
      1
    2 4 3
  + 1 7 8
  ───────
        1
```
3 ones + 8 ones
= 11 ones
= 1 ten 1 one

Step 2 Add the tens.
Regroup the tens.
```
    1 1
    2 4 3
  + 1 7 8
  ───────
      2 1
```
1 ten + 4 tens + 7 tens
= 12 tens
= 1 hundred 2 tens

Step 3 Add the hundreds.
```
    1 1
    2 4 3
  + 1 7 8
  ───────
    4 2 1
```
1 hundred + 2 hundreds +
1 hundred
= 4 hundreds

Find the sum.

1 The sum of 5 and 4 is ____ .

2 The sum of 3 and 15 is ____ .

3 The sum of 78 and 21 is ____ .

4 The sum of 96 and 123 is ____ .

Add.

5 813 + 172 = ____

6 654 + 312 = ____

7 508 + 271 = ____

Add.

8 635 + 249 = ____

9 188 + 396 = ____

10 217 + 397 = ____

Addition Without Regrouping

Lesson Objective

- Add greater numbers without regrouping.

Vocabulary
sum

Learn **Use base-ten blocks and a place-value chart to find the sum.**

Find the **sum** of 1,482 and 7,516.

Thousands	Hundreds	Tens	Ones

The sum of 1,482 and 7,516 is 8,998.

> When you add numbers, the answer is the sum of the numbers.

Step 1
Add the ones.

$$\begin{array}{r} 1,48\boxed{2} \\ +\ 7,51\boxed{6} \\ \hline \boxed{8} \end{array}$$

Step 2
Add the tens.

$$\begin{array}{r} 1,4\boxed{8}2 \\ +\ 7,5\boxed{1}6 \\ \hline \boxed{9}8 \end{array}$$

Step 3
Add the hundreds.

$$\begin{array}{r} 1,\boxed{4}82 \\ +\ 7,\boxed{5}16 \\ \hline \boxed{9}98 \end{array}$$

Step 4
Add the thousands.

$$\begin{array}{r} \boxed{1},482 \\ +\ \boxed{7},516 \\ \hline \boxed{8},998 \end{array}$$

Guided Learning

Find the missing numbers.

1 The sum of 2,653 and 3,302 is [   ] .

Thousands		Hundreds	Tens	Ones
2	,	6	5	3
+ 3	,	3	0	2
[ ]	,	[ ]	[ ]	[ ]

Add. Use base-ten blocks to help you.

2
```
   1, 6 9 3
 + 5, 2 0 4
```
[   ]

3
```
   4, 0 2 5
 +    3 6 4
```
[   ]

4
```
   7, 1 4 3
 + 1, 6 0 2
```
[   ]

5
```
   2, 7 0 0
 + 3, 2 9 5
```
[   ]

Let's Practice

Add. Use base-ten blocks to help you.

1 The sum of 436 and 9,210 is [   ] .

2 The sum of 2,421 and 6,308 is [   ] .

3 The sum of 5,668 and 3,020 is [   ] .

ON YOUR OWN

**Go to Workbook A:
Practice 1, pages 45–48**

3.2 Addition with Regrouping in Hundreds

Lesson Objective

- Add greater numbers with regrouping in hundreds.

Vocabulary
regroup

Learn **Use base-ten blocks and a place-value chart to regroup when you add.**

$1,200 + 2,900 = ?$

Thousands	Hundreds	Tens	Ones

Step 1
Add the hundreds.

$$\begin{array}{r} \overset{1}{1,}200 \\ +\ 2,900 \\ \hline 100 \end{array}$$

2 hundreds
+ 9 hundreds
= 11 hundreds

Regroup the hundreds.

11 hundreds
= 1 thousand
1 hundred

Thousands	Hundreds	Tens	Ones

Step 2
Add the thousands.

$$\begin{array}{r} \overset{1}{1,}200 \\ +\ 2,900 \\ \hline 4,100 \end{array}$$

1 thousand
+ 1 thousand
+ 2 thousands
= 4 thousands

The sum of 1,200 and 2,900 is 4,100.

Guided Learning

Find the missing numbers. Use base-ten blocks to help you.

1 4,500 + 3,800 = ?

First, add the hundreds and regroup.

5 hundreds + 8 hundreds = [ ] hundreds

= [ ] thousand [ ] hundreds

Then add the thousands.

[ ] thousand + 4 thousands + 3 thousands = [ ] thousands

So, 4,500 + 3,800 = [ ].

$$\begin{array}{r} 4,500 \\ +\ 3,800 \\ \hline \end{array}$$

Add. Use base-ten blocks to help you.

2
$$\begin{array}{r} 5,300 \\ +\ 1,900 \\ \hline \end{array}$$

3
$$\begin{array}{r} 2,800 \\ +\ 1,700 \\ \hline \end{array}$$

4
$$\begin{array}{r} 7,923 \\ +\ 1,541 \\ \hline \end{array}$$

5
$$\begin{array}{r} 3,840 \\ +\ 4,720 \\ \hline \end{array}$$

Find the sum of these numbers.

6 4,800 and 4,700 [ ]

7 4,300 and 2,800 [ ]

8 3,500 and 6,500 [ ]

9 2,473 and 1,623 [ ]

Players: 4 to 6
Materials:
• hundreds cards from 100 to 900 (four sets)

Snap-a-Thousand!

STEP 1 Cut out hundreds cards from 100 to 900.
You have four cards for each number.

STEP 2 Mix up the cards.
Each player draws six cards.

STEP 3 Each player shows one card at the same time.

STEP 4 Softly say "Snap-a-Thousand" when you see two cards which add to 1,000.

Example

1,000

STEP 5 The first player to say "Snap-a-Thousand" collects the two cards.

When no more thousand pairs can be found, all players show their next card and continue the game.

STEP 6 End the game when no more cards add to 1,000.

The player who collects the most pairs wins!

WORK IN PAIRS

For each sum, find a digit that will result in regrouping in the hundreds place. Then add.

Example

$$
\begin{array}{r}
\overset{1}{4},2\,0\,0 \\
+\ 2,\boxed{?}\,0\,0 \\
\hline
\end{array}
$$

If I put 1, 2, 3, 4, 5, 6, or 7 in the box, I can't regroup the hundreds. Let me try 8 or 9.

Using the digit '8'

$$
\begin{array}{r}
\overset{1}{4},2\,0\,0 \\
+\ 2,8\,0\,0 \\
\hline
0\,0\,0
\end{array}
$$

Add the hundreds first.

$$
\begin{array}{r}
\overset{1}{4},2\,0\,0 \\
+\ 2,8\,0\,0 \\
\hline
7,0\,0\,0
\end{array}
$$

Then add the thousands.
The sum is 7,000.

Using the digit '9'

The number can be 8 or 9!

$$
\begin{array}{r}
\overset{1}{4},2\,0\,0 \\
+\ 2,9\,0\,0 \\
\hline
1\,0\,0
\end{array}
$$

Add the hundreds first.

$$
\begin{array}{r}
\overset{1}{4},2\,0\,0 \\
+\ 2,9\,0\,0 \\
\hline
7,1\,0\,0
\end{array}
$$

Then add the thousands.
The sum is 7,100.

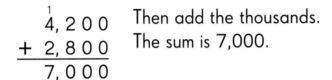

1
$$
\begin{array}{r}
5,\boxed{}\,0\,0 \\
+\ 2,6\,0\,0 \\
\hline
\end{array}
$$

2
$$
\begin{array}{r}
2,4\,0\,0 \\
+\ 3,\boxed{}\,0\,0 \\
\hline
\end{array}
$$

3
$$
\begin{array}{r}
6,8\,0\,0 \\
+\ 2,\boxed{}\,0\,0 \\
\hline
\end{array}
$$

Let's Practice

Find the sum of these numbers.

1 The sum of 4,400 and 2,700 is ____.

2 The sum of 3,500 and 5,500 is ____.

3 The sum of 2,600 and 1,600 is ____.

Add. Use base-ten blocks to help you.
Find the missing numbers.

4
```
   2, 4 7 3
+  1, 6 2 3
```

5
```
   4, 5 6 1
+  2, 7 2 8
```

6
```
   4, 4 2 2
+  2, 6 1 4
```

7
```
   5, 6 7 4
+  3, 8 1 1
```

8
```
   2, 8 2 2
+  2, 7 5 3
```

9
```
   1, 4 6 2
+  3, 7 3 2
```

ON YOUR OWN

Go to Workbook A:
Practice 2, pages 49–50

3.3 Addition with Regrouping in Ones, Tens, and Hundreds

Lesson Objective

- Add greater numbers with regrouping in ones, tens, and hundreds.

Learn **Regroup more than once.**

$1,153 + 4,959 = ?$

Thousands	Hundreds	Tens	Ones

Step 1
Add the ones.

$$\begin{array}{r} 1,1\overset{1}{5}3 \\ +\ 4,959 \\ \hline 2 \end{array}$$

3 ones + 9 ones
= 12 ones

Regroup the ones.
12 ones
= 1 ten 2 ones

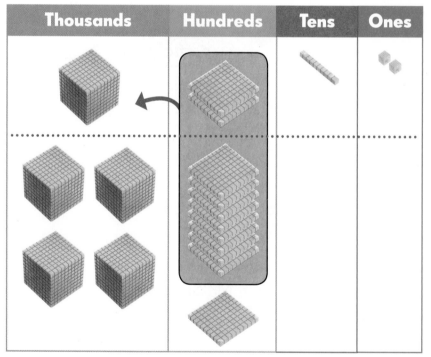

Thousands	Hundreds	Tens	Ones

Step 2
Add the tens.

$$
\begin{array}{r}
1,\ \overset{1}{1}\ \boxed{\overset{1}{5}}\ 3 \\
+\ 4,\ 9\ \boxed{5}\ 9 \\
\hline
\boxed{1}\ 2
\end{array}
$$

1 ten + 5 tens
+ 5 tens
= 11 tens

Regroup the tens.
11 tens
= 1 hundred 1 ten

Thousands	Hundreds	Tens	Ones

Step 3
Add the hundreds.

$$
\begin{array}{r}
\overset{1}{1},\ \boxed{\overset{1}{1}}\ \overset{1}{5}\ 3 \\
+\ 4,\ \boxed{9}\ 5\ 9 \\
\hline
\boxed{1}\ 1\ 2
\end{array}
$$

1 hundred
+ 1 hundred
+ 9 hundreds
= 11 hundreds

Regroup the hundreds.
11 hundreds
= 1 thousand
   1 hundred

Continued on next page

Thousands	Hundreds	Tens	Ones

The sum of 1,153 and 4,959 is 6,112.

Step 4
Add the thousands.

$$
\begin{array}{r}
\overset{1}{1,}\ \overset{1}{1}\ \overset{1}{5}\ 3 \\
+\ 4,\ 9\ 5\ 9 \\
\hline
6,\ 1\ 1\ 2
\end{array}
$$

1 thousand
+ 1 thousand
+ 4 thousands
= 6 thousands

Guided Learning

Add. Use base-ten blocks to help you.

1
$$
\begin{array}{r}
3,6\ 2\ 8 \\
+\ 1,7\ 9\ 5 \\
\hline
\end{array}
$$

2
$$
\begin{array}{r}
5,3\ 4\ 8 \\
+\ 3,7\ 9\ 2 \\
\hline
\end{array}
$$

Solve.

3 One year, the population of Crystal Town is 7,325.
Within the same year, 1,796 people move into the town.
How many people are now in Crystal Town?

4 Mr. Streep makes 4,728 dinner rolls in a day.
Mr. Wu makes 1,584 more dinner rolls than Mr. Streep.
How many dinner rolls does Mr. Wu make?

Let's Practice

Add. Use base-ten blocks to help you.

1 The sum of 3,562 and 4,729 is [   ] .

2 The sum of 6,185 and 2,847 is [   ] .

3 8,943 + 268 = [   ]

4 1,628 + 4,586 = [   ]

Solve.

5 Cathy and Jordan take a walk through the forest.
Cathy takes Route A and Jordan takes Route B.
There are 3 places where Route A and Route B cross.
They agree to meet at each place to add the two numbers
that they see along the way.
Find the three answers. [   ] [   ] [   ]

ON YOUR OWN

Go to Workbook A:
Practice 3, pages 51–54

Look at the addition problems. Explain the error in each.

Example

```
    3, 4 6 7
+   1, 9 3 2
    4, 3 9 9
```

Error: The hundreds were not regrouped into thousands and hundreds.

```
    7, 5 2 9
+   2, 4 6 1
    9, 9 8 0
```

Error: The ones were not regrouped into tens and ones.

1
```
    5, 8 6 9
+   1, 4 2 5
    4, 4 4 4
```

2
```
    3, 5 7 3
+   1, 6 4 5
    4, 1 1 8
```

List the steps for adding these two numbers.

Example

```
     1
    2 3 4
+   4 7 5
    7 0 9
```

Step 1
Add 4 ones and 5 ones to get 9 ones.

Step 2
Add 3 tens and 7 tens to get 10 tens.

Step 3
Regroup 10 tens into 1 hundred and 0 tens.

Step 4
Add 1 hundred, 2 hundreds, and 4 hundreds to get 7 hundreds.

3
```
    4, 2 6 7
+   2, 9 1 5
```

Put On Your Thinking Cap!

PROBLEM SOLVING

Find the sum of the numbers.
Use number bonds to help you find a number pattern.

Example

$320 + 182 + 260 + 242 + 160 + 342 + 360 +$
$142 + 190 + 312 = ?$

$320 + 182 = 500 + 2$
$260 + 242 = 500 + 2$
$160 + 342 = 500 + 2$
$360 + 142 = 500 + 2$
$190 + 312 = 500 + 2$

Look for a pattern.

Five 500s + five 2s
$= 2,500 + 10$
$= 2,510$

1   $360 + 645 + 720 + 285 + 430 + 575 +$
$810 + 195 = ?$

ON YOUR OWN

**Go to Workbook A:
Put On Your Thinking Cap!
pages 55–58**

Chapter Wrap Up

Study Guide

You have learned...

BIG IDEA

► Greater numbers can be added the same way 2-digit numbers are added, with or without regrouping.

Addition up to 10,000

Without Regrouping

2,315 + 1,231 = 3,546

```
   2, 3 1 5
+  1, 2 3 1
   3, 5 4 6
```

Step 1 Add the ones.
5 ones + 1 one
= 6 ones

Step 2 Add the tens.
1 ten + 3 tens
= 4 tens

Step 3 Add the hundreds.
3 hundreds
+ 2 hundreds
= 5 hundreds

Step 4 Add the thousands.
2 thousands
+ 1 thousand
= 3 thousands

With Regrouping

1,434 + 4,567 = 6,001

```
    1  1  1
   1, 4 3 4
+  4, 5 6 7
   6, 0 0 1
```

Step 1 Add the ones and regroup.
4 ones + 7 ones
= 11 ones
= 1 ten 1 one

Step 2 Add the tens and regroup.
1 ten + 3 tens + 6 tens
= 10 tens
= 1 hundred 0 tens

Step 3 Add the hundreds and regroup.
1 hundred + 4 hundreds
+ 5 hundreds
= 10 hundreds
= 1 thousand 0 hundreds

Step 4 Add the thousands.
1 thousand + 1 thousand
+ 4 thousands
= 6 thousands

Chapter Review/Test

Vocabulary
Choose the correct word.

> sum
> addition
> regroup

1 When you ⬚ 23 ones, you get 2 tens 3 ones.

2 When you add two or more numbers, the answer is the ⬚ .

Concepts and Skills
Add.

3
```
  3, 1 1 2
+    6 3 5
─────────
```

4
```
  5, 6 1 8
+ 2, 0 4 5
─────────
```

5
```
  2, 5 7 3
+ 1, 9 8 9
─────────
```

6
```
  6, 7 2 5
+ 2, 8 0 5
─────────
```

Find the sum.

7 The sum of 6,213 and 2,418 is ⬚ .

8 The sum of 4,283 and 2,974 is ⬚ .

Problem Solving
Solve.

9 Baker Elliot bakes 2,925 buns in three months.
He bakes 1,861 fewer buns than Baker Susan.
How many buns does Baker Susan bake? ⬚

10 3,695 children visit the art museum in January.
816 more children visit the art museum in February than in January.
How many children visit the museum in February? ⬚

4 Subtraction up to 10,000

Lessons

BIG IDEA

▶ Greater numbers can be subtracted with or without regrouping.

Finding the difference

70 − 12 = ?

$$\begin{array}{r} \overset{6}{\cancel{7}}\,{}^{1}0 \\ -\ 1\ 2 \\ \hline 5\ 8 \end{array}$$ ← difference

The difference between 70 and 12 is 58.

Subtracting 3-digit numbers without regrouping

859 − 325 = ?

Step 1 Subtract the ones.

$$\begin{array}{r} 8\ 5\ 9 \\ -\ 3\ 2\ 5 \\ \hline 4 \end{array}$$

Step 2 Subtract the tens.

$$\begin{array}{r} 8\ 5\ 9 \\ -\ 3\ 2\ 5 \\ \hline 3\ 4 \end{array}$$

Step 3 Subtract the hundreds.

$$\begin{array}{r} 8\ 5\ 9 \\ -\ 3\ 2\ 5 \\ \hline 5\ 3\ 4 \end{array}$$

Subtracting 3-digit numbers with regrouping

$$\begin{array}{r} \overset{4}{\cancel{5}}\ {}^{1}\overset{1}{\cancel{2}}\,{}^{1}3 \\ -\ 1\ 4\ 8 \\ \hline 3\ 7\ 5 \end{array}$$

Step 1 Regroup the tens and ones. Subtract the ones.

Step 2 Regroup the hundreds and tens. Subtract the tens.

Step 3 Subtract the hundreds.

✔ **Quick Check**

Find the difference.
Subtract.

1 The difference between 162 and 29 is [ ].

2 368 − 153 = [ ]

3 714 − 359 = [ ]

4.1 Subtraction Without Regrouping

Lesson Objective

- Use base-ten blocks to subtract without regrouping.

Vocabulary
difference

Learn **Use base-ten blocks and a place-value chart to find the difference .**

Find the difference between 4,368 and 1,254.

Thousands	Hundreds	Tens	Ones

Thousands	Hundreds	Tens	Ones

The difference between 4,368 and 1,254 is 3,114.

Step 1
Subtract the ones.

$$\begin{array}{r} 4,36\boxed{8} \\ -\ 1,25\boxed{4} \\ \hline \boxed{4} \end{array}$$

Step 2
Subtract the tens.

$$\begin{array}{r} 4,3\boxed{6}8 \\ -\ 1,2\boxed{5}4 \\ \hline \boxed{1}4 \end{array}$$

Step 3
Subtract the hundreds.

$$\begin{array}{r} 4,368 \\ -\ 1,254 \\ \hline \boxed{1}14 \end{array}$$

Step 4
Subtract the thousands.

$$\begin{array}{r} \boxed{4},368 \\ -\ \boxed{1},254 \\ \hline \boxed{3},114 \end{array}$$

When you subtract numbers, the answer is the difference.

Check!

If 4,368 − 1,254 = 3,114,
then 3,114 + 1,254 should equal
4,368.
The answer is correct.

$$\begin{array}{r} 3,114 \\ +\ 1,254 \\ \hline 4,368 \end{array}$$

Guided Learning

Find the missing numbers.

1 The difference between 7,526 and 2,103 is ⬚ .

Thousands		Hundreds	Tens	Ones
7	,	5	2	6
− 2	,	1	0	3
⬚	,	⬚	⬚	⬚

Subtract. Use base-ten blocks to help you.

2
$$\begin{array}{r} 2,356 \\ -\ 1,243 \\ \hline \end{array}$$

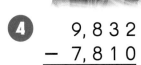

Add to check
your answers.

3
$$\begin{array}{r} 3,418 \\ -\ 3,102 \\ \hline \end{array}$$

4
$$\begin{array}{r} 9,832 \\ -\ 7,810 \\ \hline \end{array}$$

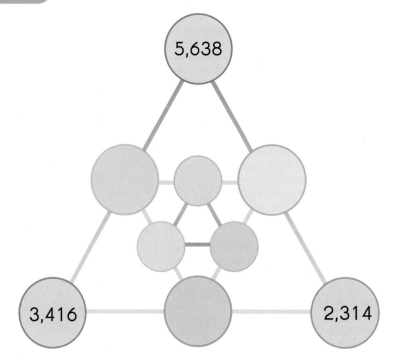

STEP 1 Use the figure provided. Choose two numbers from the figure.
Subtract the number that is less from the greater number.
Use base-ten blocks to help you.

STEP 2 Write the answer in the circle between the two numbers.

STEP 3 Repeat **STEP 1** and **STEP 2** until you fill in all the circles.

Let's Practice

Subtract.

1   3,678
     − 2,417

handwritten: 1,261   1,261

2   4,853
     − 1,121

handwritten: 3,732   3,732

3   5,942
     − 3,732

handwritten: 2,210   2,210

4   9,603
     − 5,501

handwritten: 4,102   4,102

5 The difference between 4,298 and 2,045 is ▢.

6 The difference between 5,138 and 7,459 is ▢.

7 4,786 − 2,534 = ▢

8 9,205 − 6,102 = ▢.

handwritten notes: Some in addition the same Number

handwritten calculation:
4,786
2,534
2,252

handwritten calculation:
4,298
−2,045
2253

7,459
5,138

> Add to check your answers.

ON YOUR OWN

Go to Workbook A:
Practice 1, pages 59–60

Lesson 4.2 Subtraction with Regrouping in Hundreds and Thousands

Lesson Objective

- Use base-ten blocks to subtract with regrouping.

Learn Use base-ten blocks and a place-value chart to subtract with regrouping.

$3,249 - 1,926 = ?$

Thousands	Hundreds	Tens	Ones

Step 1
Subtract the ones.

$$
\begin{array}{r}
3,2\,4\,9 \\
-\ 1,9\,2\,6 \\
\hline
3
\end{array}
$$

9 ones − 6 ones = 3 ones

Thousands	Hundreds	Tens	Ones

Step 2
Subtract the tens.

$$
\begin{array}{r}
3,2\,4\,9 \\
-\ 1,9\,2\,6 \\
\hline
2\,3
\end{array}
$$

4 tens − 2 tens = 2 tens

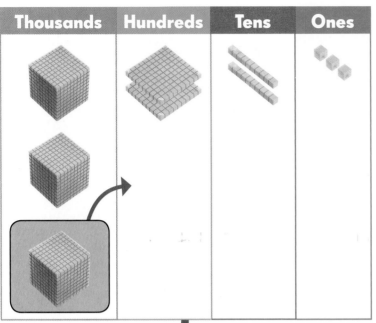

Thousands	Hundreds	Tens	Ones

$$\begin{array}{r} 3,2\,4\,9 \\ -\ 1,9\,2\,6 \\ \hline 2\,3 \end{array}$$

You cannot take away
9 hundreds from
2 hundreds. So, **regroup**
the thousands
and hundreds.

Thousands	Hundreds	Tens	Ones

Regroup.
3 thousands 2 hundreds
= 2 thousands 12 hundreds

Continued on next page

Thousands	Hundreds	Tens	Ones

Step 3
Subtract the hundreds.

$$\begin{array}{r} \overset{\overset{2}{}}{3,}\overset{1}{2}\,4\,9 \\ -\ 1,9\,2\,6 \\ \hline 3\,2\,3 \end{array}$$

12 hundreds − 9 hundreds
= 3 hundreds

Thousands	Hundreds	Tens	Ones

Step 4
Subtract
the thousands.

$$\begin{array}{r} \overset{\overset{2}{}}{3,}\overset{1}{2}\,4\,9 \\ -\ 1,9\,2\,6 \\ \hline 1,3\,2\,3 \end{array}$$

2 thousands − 1 thousand
= 1 thousand

When 1,926 is subtracted from 3,249, the difference is 1,323.

Check!

If 3,249 − 1,926 = 1,323,
then 1,323 + 1,926 should equal 3,249.
The answer is correct.

$$\begin{array}{r} \overset{1}{1,}3\,2\,3 \\ +\ 1,9\,2\,6 \\ \hline 3,2\,4\,9 \end{array}$$

Guided Learning

Regroup. Find the missing numbers.

1 7 thousands 3 hundreds = 6 thousands [ ] hundreds

2 4 thousands 1 hundred − 2 thousands 8 hundreds

= 3 thousands [ ] hundreds − 2 thousands 8 hundreds

= 1 thousand [ ] hundreds

Subtract. Use base-ten blocks to help you.

3
```
   6,2 0 0
 −   8 0 0
```
[ ]

4
```
   5,1 2 6
 − 3,4 1 2
```
[ ]

5
```
   8,4 1 5
 − 6,7 0 5
```
[ ]

Let's Practice

Add to check your answers.

Find the difference. Use base-ten blocks to help you.

1 The difference between 4,600 and 2,800 is [ ].

2 The difference between 5,678 and 742 is [ ].

3 The difference between 5,523 and 7,243 is [ ].

Subtract.

4
```
   5,2 2 1
 − 3,4 1 0
```
[ ]

5
```
   8,7 3 5
 − 2,8 1 2
```
[ ]

ON YOUR OWN

Go to Workbook A:
Practice 2, pages 61–62

Subtraction with Regrouping in Ones, Tens, Hundreds, and Thousands

Lesson Objective

- Use base-ten blocks to subtract with regrouping.

Learn **Use base-ten blocks and a place-value chart to subtract with regrouping.**

$5{,}146 - 2{,}598 = ?$

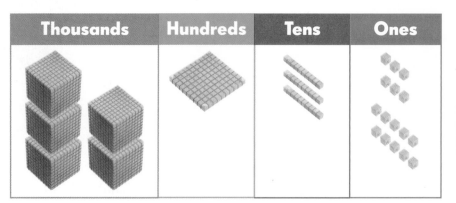

Thousands	Hundreds	Tens	Ones

$$\begin{array}{r} 5{,}146 \\ -\ 2{,}598 \\ \hline \end{array}$$

You cannot take away 8 ones from 6 ones. So, regroup the tens and ones.

Regroup.
4 tens 6 ones
= 3 tens 16 ones

Thousands	Hundreds	Tens	Ones

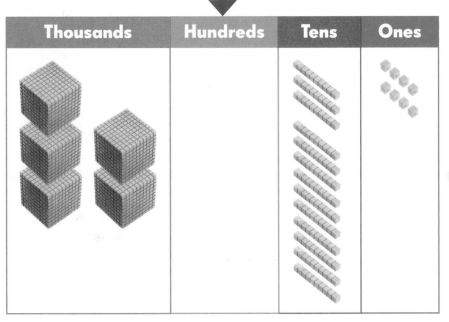

Step 1

Subtract the ones.

$$5, 1\ \overset{3}{\cancel{4}}\ ^16$$
$$-\ 2, 5\ 9\ 8$$
$$\overline{\hspace{3em}8}$$

16 ones − 8 ones
= 8 ones

$$5, 1\ \overset{3}{\cancel{4}}\ ^16$$
$$-\ 2, 5\ 9\ 8$$
$$\overline{\hspace{3em}8}$$

You cannot take
away 9 tens
from 3 tens.
So, regroup
the hundreds
and tens.

Regroup.
1 hundred 3 tens
= 0 hundreds 13 tens

Continued on next page

Lesson 4.3 Subtraction with Regrouping in Ones, Tens, Hundreds, and Thousands   **103**

Thousands	Hundreds	Tens	Ones

Step 2

Subtract the tens.

$$\begin{array}{r} {}^{0}\!\!\not{1}\;{}^{1}\!3 \\ 5,\not{1}\;\not{4}\,{}^{1}6 \\ -\;2,5\;9\,8 \\ \hline 4\,8 \end{array}$$

13 tens − 9 tens
= 4 tens

Thousands	Hundreds	Tens	Ones

$$\begin{array}{r} {}^{0}\!\!\not{1}\;{}^{1}\!3 \\ 5,\not{1}\;\not{4}\,{}^{1}6 \\ -\;2,5\;9\,8 \\ \hline 4\,8 \end{array}$$

You cannot take
away 5 hundreds
from 0 hundreds.
So, regroup the
thousands and
hundreds.

Thousands	Hundreds	Tens	Ones

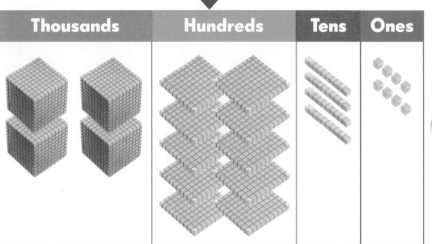

Regroup.

5 thousands 0 hundreds
= 4 thousands
   10 hundreds

Thousands	Hundreds	Tens	Ones

Step 3
Subtract the
hundreds.

$$\begin{array}{r} {}^{4}\;{}^{1}0\;{}^{1}3 \\ 5,\!1\;4\;{}^{1}6 \\ -\;2,\!5\;9\;8 \\ \hline 5\;4\;8 \end{array}$$

10 hundreds
− 5 hundreds
= 5 hundreds

Thousands	Hundreds	Tens	Ones

Step 4
Subtract the
thousands.

$$\begin{array}{r} {}^{4}\;{}^{1}0\;{}^{1}3 \\ 5,\!1\;4\;{}^{1}6 \\ -\;2,\!5\;9\;8 \\ \hline 2,\!5\;4\;8 \end{array}$$

4 thousands
− 2 thousands
= 2 thousands

The difference between 5,146 and 2,598 is 2,548.

Check!

If 5,146 − 2,598 = 2,548,
then 2,548 + 2,598 should equal 5,146.
The answer is correct.

$$\begin{array}{r} {}^{1}\;{}^{1}\;{}^{1} \\ 2,\!5\;4\;8 \\ +\;2,\!5\;9\;8 \\ \hline 5,\!1\;4\;6 \end{array}$$

Guided Learning

Regroup. Find the missing numbers.

1 5 hundreds 8 tens = 4 hundreds ▭ tens

2 9 hundreds 3 tens 2 ones − 4 hundreds 4 tens 4 ones
= 9 hundreds ▭ tens ▭ ones − 4 hundreds 4 tens 4 ones
= 8 hundreds ▭ tens 12 ones − 4 hundreds 4 tens 4 ones

Subtract. Use base-ten blocks to help you.

3
```
   5, 1 7 6
−  4, 3 7 8
  _____
   ▭
```

4
```
   6, 4 5 2
−  2, 7 8 3
  _____
   ▭
```

5
```
   8, 3 2 4
−  5, 7 8 6
  _____
   ▭
```

Let's Practice

Find the difference. Use base-ten blocks to help you.

1 The difference between 8,240 and 3,971 is ▭ .

2 The difference between 6,130 and 2,580 is ▭ .

3 The difference between 9,162 and 467 is ▭ .

4 The difference between 3,210 and 1,789 is ▭ .

5 The difference between 2,310 and 1,627 is ▭ .

6 The difference between 4,692 and 893 is ▭ .

Add to check your answers.

ON YOUR OWN

**Go to Workbook A:
Practice 3, pages 63–66**

Go for the Smallest!

Players: 2 to 4
Materials:
- seven sets of number cards from 0 to 9

STEP 1 Cut out seven sets of number cards from 0 to 9.

STEP 2 Mix up the cards. Each player turns eight cards face up.

STEP 3 Arrange your cards so that you get two 4-digit numbers.

STEP 4 Subtract the numbers. The player with the least difference scores 5 points. Play three rounds.

The player with the most points wins!

 **Subtraction Across Zeros**

Lesson Objectives

- Use base-ten blocks to subtract across zeros.
- Write subtraction number sentences.
- Solve subtraction word problems.

^{Learn} **Use base-ten blocks when subtracting across zeros.**

2,000 − 257 = ?

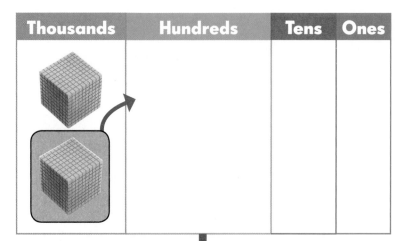

Regroup the thousands and hundreds.

Regroup.
2 thousands
= 1 thousand 10 hundreds

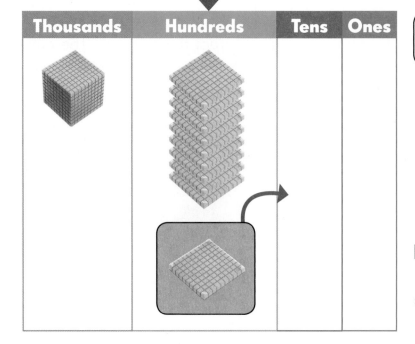

Regroup the hundreds and tens.

Regroup.
10 hundreds
= 9 hundreds 10 tens

Thousands	Hundreds	Tens	Ones
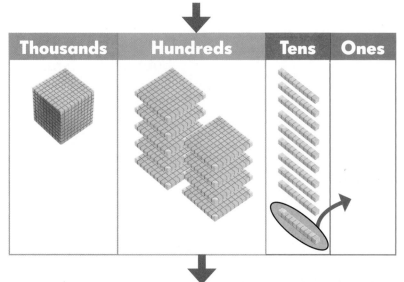			

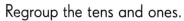

Regroup the tens and ones.

Regroup.
10 tens = 9 tens 10 ones

Thousands	Hundreds	Tens	Ones

Thousands	Hundreds	Tens	Ones

Step 1
Subtract the ones.

$$
\begin{array}{r}
{\overset{1}{\cancel{2}}\,\overset{19}{\cancel{0}}\,\overset{19}{\cancel{0}}\,\overset{1}{\cancel{0}}} \\
-\quad 2\ 5\ 7 \\
\hline
3
\end{array}
$$

10 ones − 7 ones
= 3 ones

Continued on next page

Thousands	Hundreds	Tens	Ones

Step 2
Subtract the tens.

$$\begin{array}{r} 2\,\overset{1}{0}\,\overset{\overset{1}{9}}{0}\,\overset{\overset{1}{9}}{0} \\ -\quad 2\ 5\ 7 \\ \hline \quad\ 4\ 3 \end{array}$$

9 tens − 5 tens = 4 tens

Thousands	Hundreds	Tens	Ones

Step 3
Subtract the hundreds.

$$\begin{array}{r} 2\,\overset{1}{0}\,\overset{\overset{1}{9}}{0}\,\overset{\overset{1}{9}}{0} \\ -\quad 2\ 5\ 7 \\ \hline \quad 7\ 4\ 3 \end{array}$$

9 hundreds − 2 hundreds = 7 hundreds

Thousands	Hundreds	Tens	Ones

Step 4
Subtract the thousands.

$$\begin{array}{r} 2\,\overset{1}{0}\,\overset{\overset{1}{9}}{0}\,\overset{\overset{1}{9}}{0} \\ -\quad 2\ 5\ 7 \\ \hline 1,\ 7\ 4\ 3 \end{array}$$

1 thousand − 0 thousands = 1 thousand

The difference between 2,000 and 257 is 1,743.

Can you use estimation to check if your answer is accurate? Explain why or why not.

Guided Learning

Subtract. Use base-ten blocks to help you.

1
$$\begin{array}{r} 5,000 \\ -\ 3,700 \\ \hline \end{array}$$

2
$$\begin{array}{r} 6,000 \\ -\ 4,765 \\ \hline \end{array}$$

Add to check your answers.

3
$$\begin{array}{r} 8,003 \\ -\ 5,147 \\ \hline \end{array}$$

Solve.

4 Simon scores 4,000 points in a game.
Leanne scores 935 fewer points in the game than Simon.
How many points does Leanne score?

5 A store has 2,000 reams of paper and 1,726 notebooks.
How many more reams of paper than notebooks does the store have?

6 3005 types of plants are on display at a flower show.
987 plants are orchids.
How many other types of plants are there?

Players: **4 to 8**
Materials:
• Card A and Card B

Subtract the Numbers!

STEP 1 Pick one number from Card A and a greater number from Card B.

Card A
126
12
1,645
3,200

Card B
1,000
2,000
3,000
4,000

STEP 2 Subtract the number that is less from the greater number.

$$4,000 - 3,200$$

STEP 3 Play four rounds.

The group with the most correct answers wins!

Let's Practice

Subtract.

1
$$\begin{array}{r} 7,000 \\ -\ 2,840 \\ \hline \end{array}$$

2
$$\begin{array}{r} 3,0\,\cancel{1}\,0 \\ -\ 2,793 \\ \hline 7 \end{array}$$

3
$$\begin{array}{r} 2,005 \\ -\ 1,007 \\ \hline \end{array}$$

4 The difference between 7,000 and 42 is [ ].

5 The difference between 8,000 and 159 is [ ].

Solve.

6 An art school buys 1,450 ink stamps and 3,000 markers.
How many more markers than ink stamps does the school buy? [ ]

7 Sonya folds 1,000 green and red paper stars.
692 paper stars are green.
How many are red? [ ]

ON YOUR OWN

**Go to Workbook A:
Practice 4, pages 67–68**

READING AND WRITING MATH
Math Journal

Explain the errors.
Then find the correct answer.

1
```
    5, 4 0 6
 − 3, 7 9 8 ✗
    2, 3 9 2
```

2
```
    7, 2 8 5
 − 3, 4 2 9 ✗
    3, 8 6 6
```

3
```
    5, 1 2 8
 − 4, 5 3 4 ✗
    9, 6 6 2
```

CRITICAL THINKING SKILLS
Put On Your Thinking Cap!

PROBLEM SOLVING
Find the missing numbers.

1
```
    4, ▢ 8 3
 − 1, 7 2 ▢
   ▢, 8 5 7
```

2
```
    7, ▢ 5 1
 − ▢, 6 1 9
    4, 8 3 ▢
```

3
```
   ▢, 0 ▢ 0
 − 2, 6 4 3
    2, ▢ 5 7
```

4
```
    8, ▢ 4 0
 − ▢, 7 ▢ 9
    4, 2 7 ▢
```

ON YOUR OWN

Go to Workbook A:
Put On Your Thinking Cap!
pages 69–72

Chapter Wrap Up

Study Guide

You have learned...

BIG IDEA

▶ Greater numbers can be subtracted with or without regrouping.

Subtraction up to 10,000

Without Regrouping

Subtract the ones.
Subtract the tens.
Subtract the hundreds.
Subtract the thousands.

$$
\begin{array}{r}
4,663 \\
-\ 1,231 \\
\hline
3,432
\end{array}
$$

Check using addition.
If 4,663 − 1,231 = 3,432,
then 3,432 + 1,231 should equal 4,663.

$$
\begin{array}{r}
3,432 \\
+\ 1,231 \\
\hline
4,663
\end{array}
$$

With Regrouping

egroup.
,876

= 9 thousands 8 hundreds
  7 tens 6 ones

= 9 thousands 8 hundreds 6 tens
  16 ones

= 9 thousands 7 hundreds 16 tens 16 ones

= 8 thousands 17 hundreds 16 tens
  16 ones

$$
\begin{array}{r}
{}^{8}\ {}^{17}{}^{16}\ {}^{1} \\
9,876 \\
-\ 7,877 \\
\hline
1,999
\end{array}
$$

heck using addition.
 9,876 − 7,877 = 1,999,
en 1,999 + 7,877
ould equal 9,876.

$$
\begin{array}{r}
{}^{1}\ {}^{1}\ {}^{1} \\
1,999 \\
+\ 7,877 \\
\hline
9,876
\end{array}
$$

Regroup.
5,000

= 5 thousands

= 4 thousands 10 hundreds

= 4 thousands 9 hundreds 10 tens

= 4 thousands 9 hundreds 9 tens
  10 ones

$$
\begin{array}{r}
{}^{4}\ {}^{9}\ {}^{9} \\
5,000 \\
-\ 4,321 \\
\hline
679
\end{array}
$$

Check using addition.
If 5,000 − 4,321 = 679,
then 679 + 4,321
should equal 5,000.

$$
\begin{array}{r}
{}^{1}\ {}^{1}\ {}^{1} \\
679 \\
+\ 4,321 \\
\hline
5,000
\end{array}
$$

Chapter Review/Test

Vocabulary

Choose the correct word.

> subtraction sentence
>
> regroup
>
> difference

1 When you subtract numbers, the answer is the ⬚ .

2 You ⬚ thousands and hundreds when you rewrite 4 thousands as 3 thousands 10 hundreds.

3 A mathematical statement with a minus sign and an equal symbol is an example of a ⬚ .

Concepts and Skills

Subtract.

4
$$\begin{array}{r} 3,742 \\ -631 \\ \hline \end{array}$$

5
$$\begin{array}{r} 7,025 \\ -1,413 \\ \hline \end{array}$$

6
$$\begin{array}{r} 4,366 \\ -749 \\ \hline \end{array}$$

7
$$\begin{array}{r} 5,782 \\ -1,913 \\ \hline \end{array}$$

8
$$\begin{array}{r} 9,326 \\ -1,438 \\ \hline \end{array}$$

9
$$\begin{array}{r} 1,000 \\ -715 \\ \hline \end{array}$$

Problem Solving

Solve.

10 6,000 empty cans are collected in a recycling drive.
3,156 of them are crushed.
How many cans are left? ⬚

11 6,206 tickets are available for a concert.
2,078 tickets are sold.
How many tickets are still available? ⬚

5 Using Bar Models: Addition and Subtraction

BIG IDEA

▶ Bar models, addition, and subtraction can be used to solve 2-step real-world problems.

Recall Prior Knowledge

Using part–whole bar models to solve real-world problems on addition

Mrs. Jones buys a cake for $15 and has $42 left.
How much money did Mrs. Jones have at first?

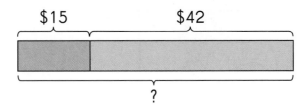

$15 + $42 = $57

Mrs. Jones had $57.

Using adding-on bar models to solve real-world problems on addition

Shawn orders 75 boxes of fruit on the first day.
He orders another 84 boxes of fruit on the second day.
How many boxes of fruit does he order on both days?

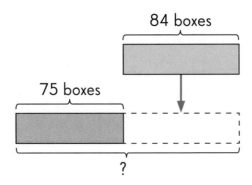

75 + 84 = 159

Shawn orders 159 boxes of fruits on both days.

Using comparison bar models to solve real-world problems on addition

Grant buys 345 fruit bars.
Ken buys 230 more fruit bars than Grant.
How many fruit bars does Ken buy?

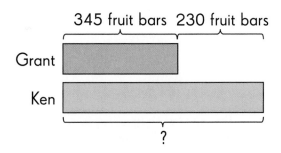

345 + 230 = 575

Ken buys 575 fruit bars.

Using part–whole bar models to solve real-world problems on subtraction

Ben has 60 baseball cards and football cards in all.
He has 24 football cards.
How many baseball cards does he have?

24 football   ? baseball
cards   cards

60 baseball and football cards

60 − 24 = 36

He has 36 baseball cards.

Using taking-away bar models to solve real-world problems on subtraction

Bob has 110 bottles of water.
He sells 28 bottles of water.
How many bottles of water does he have left?

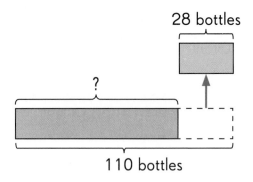

$110 - 28 = 82$

Bob has 82 bottles of water left.

Using comparison bar models to solve real-world problems on subtraction

Tanya reads 749 pages.
Michelle reads 324 fewer pages than Tanya.
How many pages does Michelle read?

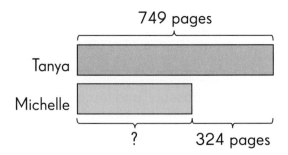

$749 - 324 = 425$

Michelle reads 425 pages.

Solve. Use bar models to help you.

1 Celeste counts 15 pictures of monkeys and 20 pictures of birds in her book. How many pictures of monkeys and birds does she count?

2 Jonathan reads 121 pages of a book on Saturday. He reads another 59 pages on Sunday. How many pages does he read in the two days?

3 An orchard has 637 apple trees. 360 of the trees grow green apples. How many of the trees grow red apples?

4 A tank holds 546 liters of water. 327 liters of water are poured out. How much water is left in the tank?

5 Sandy has $586. Sandy has $124 less than Peter. How much money does Peter have?

6 A supermarket displays 350 strawberries for sale. On display are 186 more strawberries than oranges. How many oranges are on display?

 **Real-World Problems: Addition and Subtraction**

Lesson Objective

- Use bar models to solve 2-step real-world problems on addition and subtraction.

Vocabulary
sum
difference
bar model

Use bar models and addition or subtraction to solve 2-step real-world problems.

Nancy and Sue sold tickets for a concert.
Nancy sold 3,450 tickets.
Sue sold 1,286 fewer tickets than Nancy.

a How many tickets did Sue sell?

b How many tickets did they sell in all?

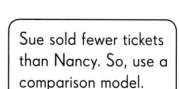

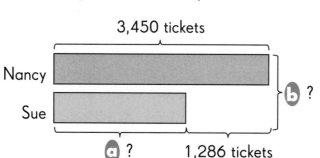

3,450 tickets

Nancy

Sue

b ?

a ?   1,286 tickets

Sue sold fewer tickets than Nancy. So, use a comparison model.

a 3,450 − 1,286 = 2,164
Sue sold 2,164 concert tickets.

b 3,450 + 2,164 = 5,614
They sold 5,614 concert tickets in all.

Check!
2,164 + 1,286 = 3,450
5,614 − 2,164 = 3,450
The answers are correct.

Guided Learning

Solve. Use bar models to help you.

1 A computer costs $1,950.
It costs $250 less than a television set.

  a How much does the television set cost?

  b How much do both items cost in all?

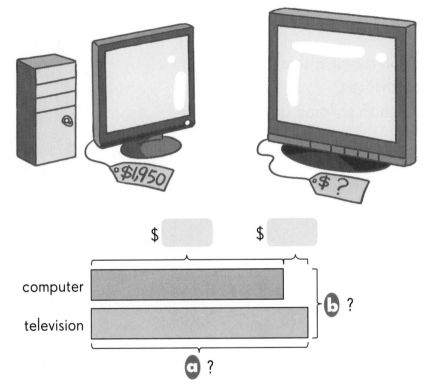

$ [　　] $ [　　]

computer [　　　　　　] **b** ?

television [　　　　　　]

  a ?

a $ [　　] [ ] $ [　　] = $ [　　]

The television set costs $ [　　].

b $ [　　] [ ] $ [　　] = $ [　　]

Both items cost $ [　　] in all.

The computer costs less than the television set. So, use a comparison model.

2 A school has 720 girls.
It has 250 more boys than girls.
How many children attend the school?

First, find the number of boys in the school.

3 5,099 passengers are on a cruise ship.
1,825 passengers are children.
How many more adults than children are on the ship?

What do you have to find first?

4 A farm has 1,263 chicks and hens.
814 of them are chicks.
How many fewer hens than chicks does the shelter have?

Check your answers.

5 Theater A has 3,460 seats.
Theater B has 290 fewer seats than Theater A.
What is the total number of seats in both theaters?

Let's Explore!

WORK IN PAIRS

STEP 1 Think of two numbers less than 50.

9 and 4

12 and 7

STEP 2 Find the sum and difference of the pair of numbers.

9 + 4 = 13
9 − 4 = 5

12 + 7 = 19
12 − 7 = 5

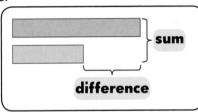

sum

difference

STEP 3 Add the sum and difference of the pair of numbers.
Compare this with the greater number in the pair.

13 + 5 = 18

19 + 5 = 24

Compare 18 and 9.

Compare 24 and 12.

STEP 4 Repeat **STEP 1** to **STEP 3** with two other pairs of numbers.

STEP 5 Do you see a pattern? Explain your answer.

Let's Practice

Solve. Use bar models to help you.

1 The gymnastic teacher pays $240 for new playground equipment.
The Science teacher pays $85 more for new laboratory equipment.

a How much does the Science teacher pay?

b How much do they pay in all?

2 Sarah travels 750 miles.
Quinn travels 125 miles more than Sarah.

a How many miles does Quinn travel?

b How many miles do they travel in all?

3 1,235 people attend a dolphin show.
275 fewer people attend a bird show.
How many people attend both shows?

4 Two trucks are carrying a total load of 2,361 oranges.
The first truck carries 886 oranges.
How many more oranges does the second truck
carry than the first truck?

For each bar model, make up a 2-step real-world problem. Then solve.

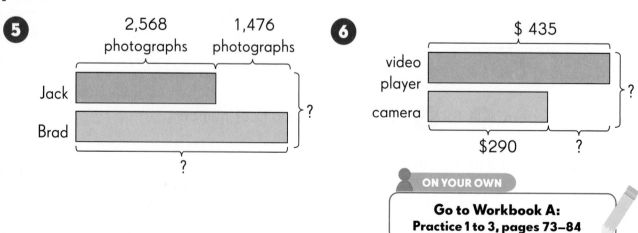

5
2,568 photographs   1,476 photographs

Jack

Brad

?

?

6
$ 435

video player

camera

$290   ?

?

ON YOUR OWN

**Go to Workbook A:
Practice 1 to 3, pages 73–84**

Put On Your Thinking Cap!

PROBLEM SOLVING

A farm has 4 kinds of animals and 8 in all.
Some of the animals have 2 legs and some have 4 legs.
The animals have 20 legs altogether.
How many of the animals have 4 legs?
Name the animals that could be under the bushes.

Start by giving
2 legs to each animal.

Remember to add up
to 20 legs in all.

[   ] of the animals have 4 legs.

The farm animals could be [   ], [   ], [   ], and [   ].

ON YOUR OWN

**Go to Workbook A:
Put On Your Thinking Cap!
pages 87–88**

Chapter Wrap Up

Study Guide

You have learned...

> **Using Bar Models: Addition and Subtraction**

> **Solve 2-Step Real-World Problems**

Addition

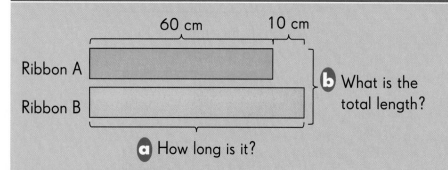

a 60 + 10 = 70
Ribbon B is 70 centimeters long.

b 60 + 70 = 130
The total length of ribbons A and B is 130 centimeters.

Subtraction

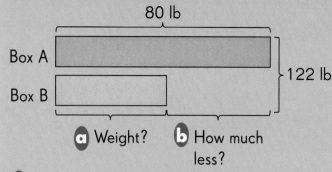

a 122 − 80 = 42
The weight of Box B is 42 pounds.

b 80 − 42 = 38
The weight of Box B is 38 pounds less than the weight of Box A.

▶ Bar models, addition, and subtraction can be used to solve 2-step real-world problems.

Addition and Subtraction

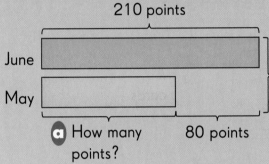

210 points

June

May

b What is the total score?

a How many points?

80 points

a 210 − 80 = 130
May scored 130 points.

b 210 + 130 = 340
Both girls scored 340 points in all.

Chapter Review/Test

Vocabulary
Choose the correct word.

bar model
sum
difference

1 A ☐ helps you to visualize a problem in pictorial form.

2 The answer to an addition problem is called the ☐.

3 The answer to a subtraction problem is called the ☐.

Concepts and Skills
Find the missing numbers in the bar models.

4
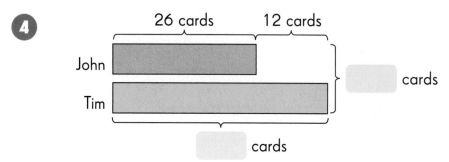

5
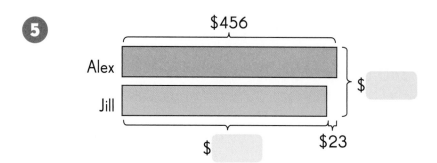

6
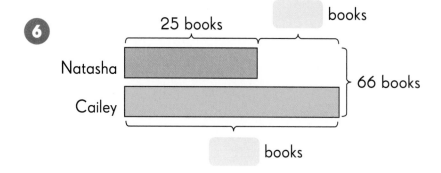

7

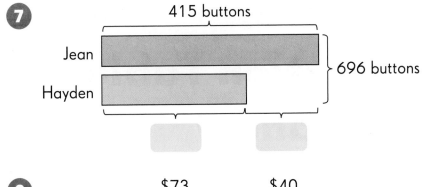

415 buttons

Jean

Hayden

696 buttons

8

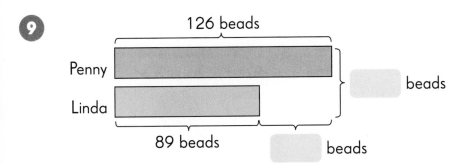

$73 $40

Book X

Book Y

$

$

9

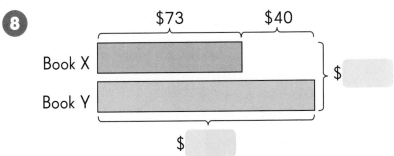

126 beads

Penny

Linda

beads

89 beads

beads

Problem Solving
Solve. Use bar models to help you.

10 A library has 3,250 fiction books.
It has 1,789 non-fiction books.

a How many more fiction than non-fiction books does the library have?

b How many fiction and non-fiction books does the library have in all?

11 315 fans of the home team are at a hockey game.
The visiting team has 28 fewer fans than the home team at the game.
How many fans are at the game in all?

Multiplication Tables of 6, 7, 8, and 9

Jenny's marker lands on the number '3'. If you use the multiplication table of 5, Jenny will call out 3 times 5 is '15'.

What number will Jenny call out if you use the multiplication table of 6?

Lessons

BIG IDEA

▶ Many models can be used to multiply.

Recall Prior Knowledge

Multiplication as equal groups

3 twos = 3 groups of 2   4 fives = 4 groups of 5

5 tens = 5 groups of 10

Multiplication as repeated addition

2 + 2 + 2 = 6

3 × 2 = 6

4 + 4 + 4 + 4 + 4 = 20

5 × 4 = 20

Multiplying as skip counting

Skip counting by 2

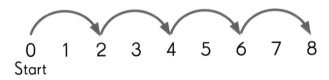

0   1   2   3   4   5   6   7   8
Start

4 × 2 = 8

Using multiplication facts you know to find other multiplication facts

6 × 3 = 5 groups of 3 + 1 group of 3
        = 15 + 3
        = 18

8 × 4 = 10 groups of 4 − 2 groups of 4
        = 40 − 8
        = 32

Multiplying numbers in any order

7 × 5 is the same as 5 × 7.
7 × 5 = 35
So, 5 × 7 = 35.

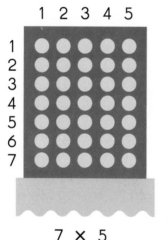
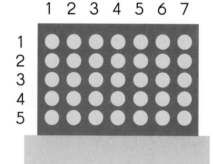

7 × 5   5 × 7

Dividing by sharing equally

Divide 15 circles into 3 equal groups.
How many circles does each group have?

15 ÷ 3 = 5

Each group has 5 circles.

Dividing by grouping

Divide 12 circles into groups so that each group has 2 circles.
How many groups are there?

$12 \div 2 = 6$

There are 6 groups.

Even and odd numbers

Even numbers can be divided into groups of 2.
4 and 10 are even numbers.

4 $\longrightarrow$ 2 groups of 2
10 $\longrightarrow$ 5 groups of 2

Odd numbers can be divided into groups of 2 with remainder 1.
5 and 11 are odd numbers.

5 $\longrightarrow$ 2 groups of 2 and 1
11 $\longrightarrow$ 5 groups of 2 and 1

Dividing using related multiplication facts

$50 \div 5 = ?$
$10 \times 5 = 50$
So, $50 \div 5 = 10$.

Multiplying and dividing in real-world problems

1 Howard arranges 4 chairs in a row. There are 9 rows.
How many chairs are there in all?

9 × 4 = 36

There are 36 chairs in all.

2 Shelly cooks 24 eggs. She puts 3 eggs on each plate.
How many plates does she use?

24 ÷ 3 = 8

She uses 8 plates.

✔ Quick Check

Find the missing numbers.

1

4 twos = [ ] groups of [ ]

2

[ ] + [ ] + [ ] + [ ] + [ ] = [ ] × 2

= [ ]

Skip-count. Find the missing numbers.

3

[ ] [ ] 9 12 [ ] [ ] 21 24 [ ] [ ]

Find the missing numbers.

4 8 × 2 = 10 groups of 2 − ⬚ groups of 2

= ⬚ − ⬚

= ⬚

5

⬚ × ⬚ = 5 × 4

= ⬚

Write *odd* or *even*.

6 11 ⬚

7 16 ⬚

Find the missing numbers.

8 15 ÷ 3 = ?

⬚ × 3 = 15

So, 15 ÷ 3 = ⬚ .

9 36 ÷ 4 = ?

⬚ × 4 = 36

So, 36 ÷ 4 = ⬚ .

Solve.

10 Angie has 10 pretzels. She puts them equally into 2 bags. How many pretzels does each bag contain? ⬚

11 There are 20 students. A van can seat 10 students. How many vans does Mrs. Smith need if she wants to take all the students to the park? ⬚

12 Sheena has 9 display cases in her shop. She puts 10 scarves in each case. How many scarves does Sheena have? ⬚

Lesson 6.1 Multiplication Properties

Lesson Objective

• Use multiplication properties.

Learn Use number lines to multiply.

This **number line** shows 1 skip of 3.

skip

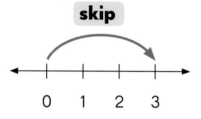

0 1 2 3

The number line shows 1 group of 3 = 1 × 3

= 3.

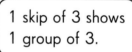

1 skip of 3 shows 1 group of 3.

This number line shows 2 skips of 3.

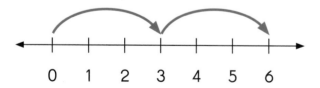

0 1 2 3 4 5 6

The number line shows 2 groups of 3 = 2 × 3

= 6.

On a number line that shows a multiplication fact, the skips show the number of equal groups.

2 skips of 3 shows 2 groups of 3.

Guided Learning

Look at each number line. Express as a multiplication fact.

1

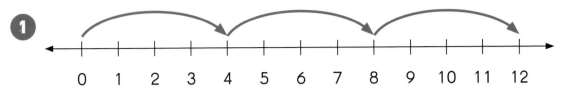

$$\boxed{} \times \boxed{} = \boxed{}$$

2

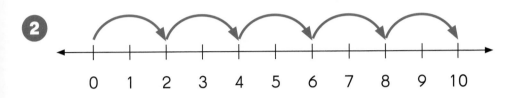

$$\boxed{} \times \boxed{} = \boxed{}$$

Express the multiplication fact on each number line.

3 $6 \times 2 = 12$

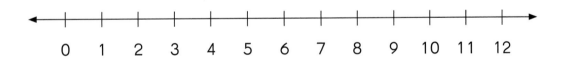

4 $3 \times 5 = 15$

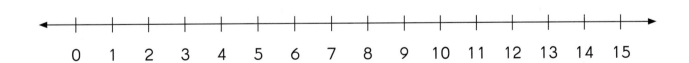

Let's Explore!

WORK IN PAIRS

Show two multiplication facts that equal 24.
Use number lines to help you.

Example

$8 \times 3 = 24$

1   □ × □ = 24

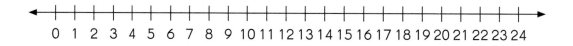

2   □ × □ = 24

Numbers can be multiplied in any order.

Using **dot paper**

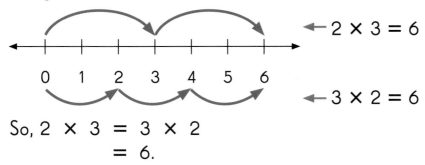

2 groups of 3 or 2 × 3   3 groups of 2 or 3 × 2

Using a number line

$2 \times 3 = 6$

0 1 2 3 4 5 6

$3 \times 2 = 6$

So, 2 × 3 = 3 × 2
         = 6.

Changing the order of numbers in a multiplication sentence does not change the answer. This is called the **commutative property** of multiplication.

Guided Learning

Find the missing numbers.

5 6 × 3 = [____]   So, 3 × [____] = [____].

6 8 × 5 = [____]   So, 5 × [____] = [____].

Show 5 × 3 = 15 and 3 × 5 = 15. Use the number line provided.

7

0 1 2 3 4 5 6 7 8 9 10 11 12 13 14 15

Using dot paper

3 groups of 1 or 3 × 1

4 groups of 1 or 4 × 1

Using a number line

3 groups of 1

3 × 1 = 3

4 groups of 1

4 × 1 = 4

1 × 3 = 3
3 × 1 = 3
So, 1 × 3 = 3 × 1.

1 × 4 = 4
4 × 1 = 4
So, 1 × 4 = 4 × 1.

Any number multiplied by 1 equals that number.
This is called the **multiplicative property of one**.

Guided Learning

Look at each number line. Express as a multiplication fact.

8

```
  0   1   2   3   4   5   6
```

[ ] × [ ] = [ ]

9

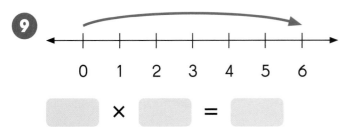

```
  0   1   2   3   4   5   6
```

[ ] × [ ] = [ ]

10 So, 1 × 6 = 6 × [ ].

= [ ]

Find the missing numbers.

11

1 × [ ] = 5

5 × [ ] = [ ]

Complete the multiplication sentences. Use the numbers provided.

12 ▢ × ▢ = ▢

13 ▢ × ▢ = ▢

ᴸᵉᵃʳⁿ **Multiply by 0.**

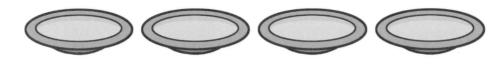

There are 4 empty plates, which means there are 4 groups of nothing.

So, $4 \times 0 = 0$.

$4 \times 0 = 0$
So, $0 \times 4 = 0$.

Any number multiplied by 0 equals 0.
This is called the **multiplicative property of zero**.

Guided Learning

Find the missing numbers.

14

▢ × ▢ = ▢

▢ × ▢ = ▢

Find the missing numbers.

15 $0 \times \boxed{} = \boxed{}$

16 $\boxed{} \times \boxed{} = 0$

Learn **Numbers can be grouped and multiplied in any order.**

$2 \times 2 \times 5 = ?$

Method 1

Step 1   Multiply the first two numbers.

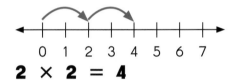

2 × 2 = 4

Step 2   Multiply the last number by the answer in Step 1.

4 × 5 = 20

So, **2** × **2** × 5 = **4** × 5

$\qquad\qquad\qquad = 20.$

Continued on next page

$2 \times 2 \times 5 = ?$

Method 2

Step 1   Multiply the last two numbers.

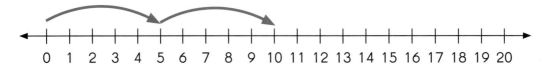

2 × 5 = 10

Step 2   Multiply the first number by the answer in Step 1.

$2 \times \mathbf{10} = 20$

So, $2 \times \mathbf{2} \times \mathbf{5} = 2 \times \mathbf{10}$
$\qquad\qquad\quad = 20.$

What do you notice about your answers?

2 × **2** × 5 = 20
2 × **2** × **5** = 20

In both methods, you get the same answer.

Changing the way numbers in a multiplication sentence are grouped and multiplied does not change the answer. This is called the **associative property** of multiplication.

Guided Learning

Multiply. Use the number lines provided.

17 5 × 2 × 3 = ?

Method 1

Step 1 Multiply the first two numbers.

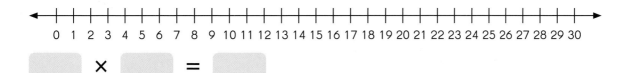

[ ] × [ ] = [ ]

Step 2 Multiply the last number by the answer in Step 1.

[ ] × [ ] = [ ]

So, **5** × **2** × 3 = [ ] × [ ]

= [ ] .

Method 2

Step 1 Multiply the last two numbers.

[ ] × [ ] = [ ]

Step 2 Multiply the first number by the answer in Step 1.

[ ] × [ ] = [ ]

So, 5 × **2** × **3** = [ ] × [ ]

= [ ] .

Complete.
Find the missing numbers. Use the answers from
Exercise 17 on page 147.

18

19 4 × 2 × 2 = ?

Method 1

Step 1   4 × 2 = [ ]

Step 2   [ ] × 2 = [ ]

Method 2

Step 1   2 × 2 = [ ]

Step 2   4 × [ ] = [ ]

So, 4 × 2 × 2 = [ ] .

Find the missing numbers.

20 8 × 7 = [ ] × 2 × 7

21 5 × 6 = 5 × 3 × [ ]

22 [ ] × 3 × [ ] = 18

23 2 × [ ] × [ ] = 32

Let's Practice

Complete each multiplication fact. Then show on each number line.

1 3 × 3 = [ ]

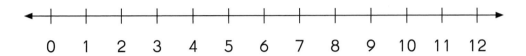

0 1 2 3 4 5 6 7 8 9 10 11 12

2 5 × 2 = [ ]

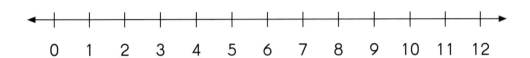

0 1 2 3 4 5 6 7 8 9 10 11 12

Look at each number line. Then express as a multiplication fact.

3

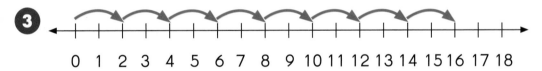

0 1 2 3 4 5 6 7 8 9 10 11 12 13 14 15 16 17 18

[ ] × [ ] = [ ]

4

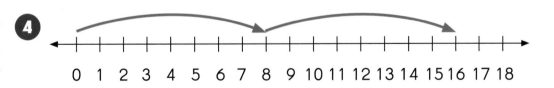

0 1 2 3 4 5 6 7 8 9 10 11 12 13 14 15 16 17 18

[ ] × [ ] = [ ]

Find the missing numbers.

5 $5 \times \boxed{} = \boxed{} \times 5$
$= 5$

6 $\boxed{} \times 1 = 1 \times \boxed{}$
$= 8$

7 $\boxed{} \times 7 = 7 \times \boxed{}$
$= 0$

8 $6 \times 0 = \boxed{} \times 6$
$= \boxed{}$

9 $2 \times 2 \times 3 = \boxed{} \times \boxed{}$
$= \boxed{}$

10 $12 \times 3 = \boxed{} \times 6 \times 3$

11 $3 \times 8 = 3 \times 2 \times \boxed{}$

ON YOUR OWN

Go to Workbook A:
Practice 1, pages 93–96

Lesson 6.2 Multiply by 6

Lesson Objectives

- Understand multiplication by using array models.
- Practice multiplication facts of 6.

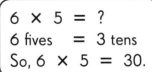

Vocabulary
array model

Learn **Use array models to show multiplication facts.**

Jasper cuts out 5 shapes.
He counts the number of sides on each shape.
There are 6 sides on each shape.
What is the total number of sides of all 5 shapes?

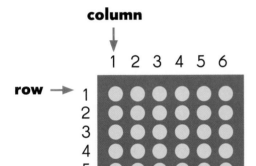

This is an array model.

There are 5 rows of 6 dots.

$5 \times 6 = 6 \times 5$
$\qquad = 30$

The total number of sides is 30.

$5 \times 6 \quad = ?$
$5 \text{ rows of } 6 = 30$

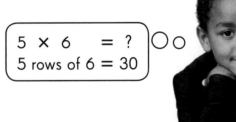

$6 \times 5 = ?$
$6 \text{ fives} \quad = 3 \text{ tens}$
So, $6 \times 5 = 30$.

A dot paper is an **array model**.
The dots are arranged in rows and columns.
In multiplication, each row has the same number of dots.

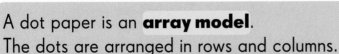

Guided Learning

Solve. Use array models to help you.

1 Ricky keeps 10 beetles.
Each beetle has 6 legs.
How many legs do the beetles have in all?

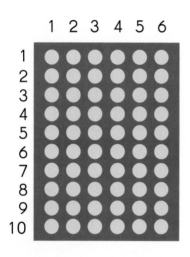

$10 \times 6 = $ ⬚ $\times$ ⬚

$= $ ⬚

The beetles have ⬚ legs in all.

2 A flower has 6 petals.
Julia buys 4 flowers.
How many petals does Julia have in all?

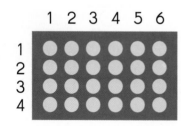

$4 \times 6 = $ ⬚ $\times$ ⬚

$= $ ⬚

Julia has ⬚ petals in all.

Use multiplication facts you know to find other multiplication facts.

$7 \times 6 = ?$

Start with 5 groups of 6.

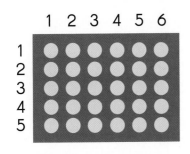

$5 \times 6 = 30$

$$7 \times 6 = 5 \text{ groups of } 6$$
$$+ \ 2 \text{ groups of } 6$$
$$= 30 + 12$$
$$= 42$$

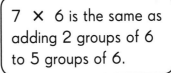

7×6 is the same as adding 2 groups of 6 to 5 groups of 6.

$$5 \times 6 = 6 \times 5$$
$$= 30$$

Continued on next page

$9 \times 6 = ?$

Start with 10 groups of 6.

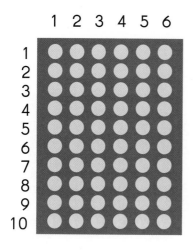

$$10 \times 6 = 60$$

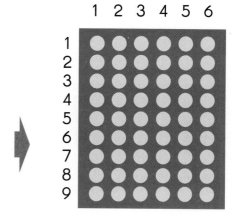

$$9 \times 6 = \text{10 groups of 6}$$
$$ - \text{1 group of 6}$$
$$= 60 - 6$$
$$= 54$$

$$10 \times 6 = 6 \times 10$$
$$= 60$$

9×6 is the same as subtracting 1 group of 6 from 10×6.

Guided Learning

Find the missing numbers. Use array models to help you.

3 6 × 6 = ?
Start with 5 groups of 6.

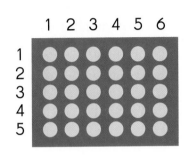

5 × 6 = [ ]

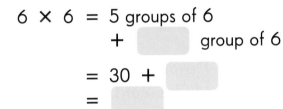

6 × 6 = 5 groups of 6
+ [ ] group of 6
= 30 + [ ]
= [ ]

4 8 × 6 = ?
Start with 10 groups of 6.

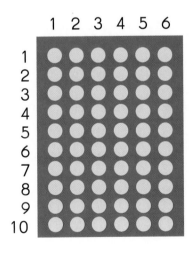

10 × 6 = [ ]

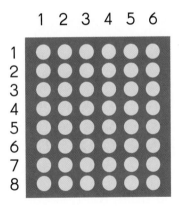

8 × 6 = 10 groups of 6
− [ ] groups of 6
= 60 − [ ]
= [ ]

Number Train!

Each player gets a number train as shown.

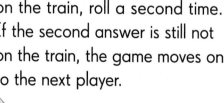

STEP 1 Player 1 chooses a face-up number card, such as 2.

STEP 2 Player 1 then rolls the number cube to get another number, such as number 6.
Player 1 then multiplies the two numbers.
$2 \times 6 = 12$
The other players check the answer.

STEP 3 If Player 1's answer is correct, he or she colors the answer on his or her number train.
If the answer is correct but not on the train, roll a second time. If the second answer is still not on the train, the game moves on to the next player.

STEP 4 Players take turns. A player gets one bonus roll with each completely colored car.

The first player to color all the numbers on the train wins!

Multiplication Table of 6

1	×	6	=	6
2	×	6	=	12
3	×	6	=	18
4	×	6	=	24
5	×	6	=	30
6	×	6	=	36
7	×	6	=	42
8	×	6	=	48
9	×	6	=	54
10	×	6	=	60

Let's Practice

Complete each skip-counting pattern.

1 6   12   18

2 24   30   36

Multiply. Use array models to help you.

3 5 × 6 =

4 6 × 6 =

5 7 × 6 =

6 8 × 6 =

7 9 × 6 =

8 10 × 6 =

9 3 × 6 =

10 5 × 6 =

ON YOUR OWN

**Go to Workbook A:
Practice 2, pages 97–100**

6.3 Multiply by 7

Lesson Objectives

- Understand multiplication by using area models.
- Practice multiplication facts of 7.

Vocabulary
area model

Learn **Use area models to show multiplication facts.**

Tracy has some craft sticks.
She makes 4 similar shapes with them.
She uses 7 craft sticks for each shape.

How many craft sticks does she use in all?

This is an **area model**.

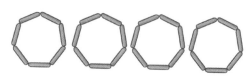

$4 \times 7 = ?$

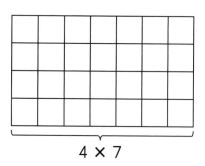

4×7

$$4 \times 7 = 7 + 7 + 7 + 7$$
$$= 28$$

4 rows of 7
$= 7 + 7 + 7 + 7$

She uses 28 craft sticks in all.

Guided Learning

Solve. Use area models to help you.

1 Jen has 3 pea pods.
Each pea pod contains 7 peas.
How many peas does Jen have in all?

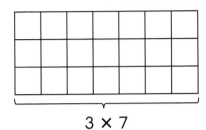

3 × 7

[ ] × [ ] = [ ] + [ ] + [ ]

= [ ]

Jen has [ ] peas in all.

2 Allyson has 5 bracelets.
Each bracelet has 7 beads.
How many beads does Allyson have in all?

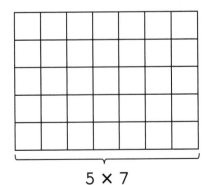

5 × 7

[ ] × [ ] = [ ] + [ ] + [ ] + [ ] + [ ]

= [ ]

Allyson has [ ] beads in all.

Use multiplication facts you know to find other multiplication facts.

$6 \times 7 = ?$

Start with 5 groups of 7.

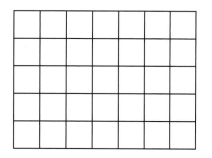

$5 \times 7 = 35$

$6 \times 7 = $ 5 groups of 7 $+$ 1 group of 7

$\qquad = 35 + 7$

$\qquad = 42$

$5 \times 7 = 7 \times 5$
$\qquad = 35$

6×7 is the same as adding 1 group of 7 to 5×7.

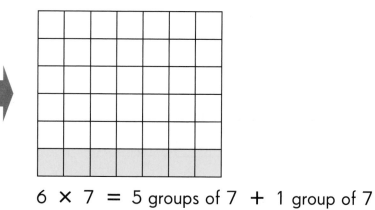

$10 \times 7 = 7 \times 10$
$\qquad = 70$

9×7 is the same as subtracting 1 group of 7 from 10×7.

$9 \times 7 = ?$

Start with 10 groups of 7.

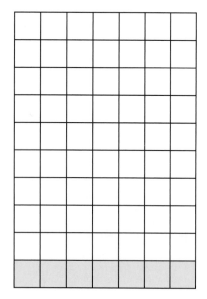

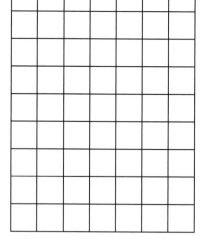

$10 \times 7 = 70$

$9 \times 7 = $ 10 groups of 7 $-$ 1 group of 7

$\qquad = 70 - 7$

$\qquad = 63$

Guided Learning

Find the missing numbers. Use area models to help you.

3 $7 \times 7 = ?$
Start with 5 groups of 7.

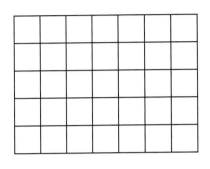 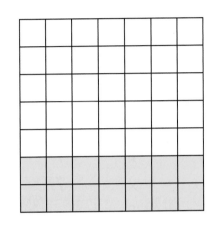

$5 \times 7 = $ [ ]

$7 \times 7 = 5$ groups of 7 $+$ [ ] groups of 7

$= 35 + $ [ ]

$= $ [ ]

4 $8 \times 7 = ?$
Start with 10 groups of 7.

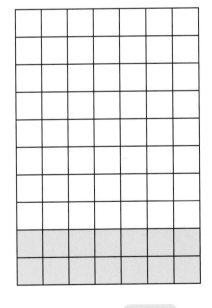 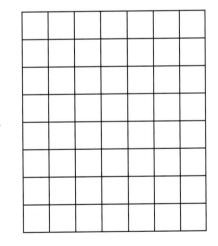

$10 \times 7 = $ [ ]

$8 \times 7 = 10$ groups of 7 $- $ [ ] groups of 7

$= $ [ ] $-$ [ ]

$= $ [ ]

Multiplication Table of 7

1	×	7	=	7
2	×	7	=	14
3	×	7	=	21
4	×	7	=	28
5	×	7	=	35
6	×	7	=	42
7	×	7	=	49
8	×	7	=	56
9	×	7	=	63
10	×	7	=	70

Let's Practice

Complete each skip-counting pattern.

1 7   14   21

2 28   35   42

Multiply.

3 4 × 7 =

4 5 × 7 =

5 6 × 7 =

6 8 × 7 =

7 9 × 7 =

8 10 × 7 =

ON YOUR OWN

Go to Workbook A:
Practice 3, pages 101–104

6.4 Multiply by 8

Lesson Objectives

- Understand multiplication by using number lines and area models.
- Practice multiplication facts of 8.

Use number lines to show multiplication facts.

At the aquarium, Hector sees 3 octopuses.
Each octopus has 8 tentacles.
How many tentacles do the octopuses have in all?

> 3 groups of 8 legs
> $= 3 \times 8$

3 skips of 8 show 3 groups of 8.

So, $3 \times 8 = 24$.

> I can also show 3×8
> in another way.
> 8 groups of $3 = 8 \times 3$

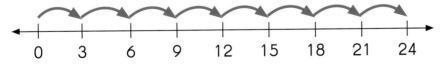

8 skips of 3 show 8 groups of 3.

So, $8 \times 3 = 24$.

Guided Learning

Look at the number line. Then express as a multiplication fact.

1

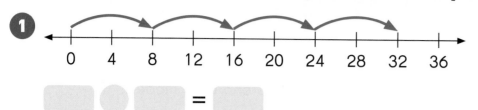

☐ ⬤ ☐ = ☐

Express the multiplication fact on the number line. Then complete.

2

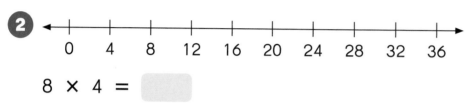

8 × 4 = ☐

Learn Use multiplication facts you know to find other multiplication facts.

Kathy has 6 spiders. Each spider has 8 legs.
How many legs do the spiders have in all.

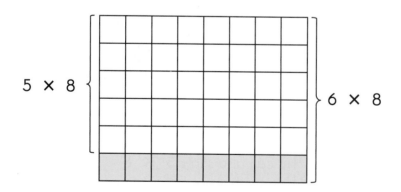

5 × 8

6 × 8

6 × 8 = 5 groups of 8 + 1 group of 8
= 40 + 8
= 48

The spiders have 48 legs in all.

5 × 8 = 8 × 5
= 40
6 × 8 is the same as adding
1 group of 8 to 5 × 8.

Guided Learning

Solve. Use the area model to help you.

3 Lily has 7 packs of paper plates.
Each pack contains 8 paper plates.
How many paper plates does Lily have in all?

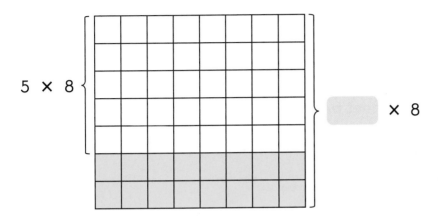

5×8 [   ] $\times 8$

$7 \times 8 = 5$ groups of 8 + [   ] groups of 8

$ = 40 +$ [   ]

$ =$ [   ]

Lily has [   ] paper plates in all.

$5 \times 8 = 8 \times 5$
$ = 40$
7×8 is the same as
adding 2 groups of 8
to 5×8.

WORKING TOGETHER **Game**

Players: 4 to 6
Materials:
- worksheets
- digit cards with numbers from 1 to 9
- multiplier cards with numbers from 6 to 8

Let's Multiply!

Each player uses the worksheet provided.

×	1	2	3	4	5	6	7	8	9
8									
7									
6									

 STEP 1 Player 1 draws a digit card and a multiplier card.

 STEP 2 Player 1 multiplies the number on the digit card by the number on the multiplier card. The other players check the answer.

6 × 8 = 48

 STEP 3 Player 1 writes the answer in the correct box on the worksheet.
The player does not write on the worksheet if the answer is incorrect.

×	1	2	3	4	5	6	7	8	9
8						48			
7									
6									

 STEP 4 Return the cards and mix them up. Players take turns to play.

The first player to fill a complete row on the worksheet wins!

Multiplication Table of 8

1	×	8	=	8
2	×	8	=	16
3	×	8	=	24
4	×	8	=	32
5	×	8	=	40
6	×	8	=	48
7	×	8	=	56
8	×	8	=	64
9	×	8	=	72
10	×	8	=	80

Let's Practice

Complete each skip-counting pattern.

1 8   16   24   ▢   ▢   ▢

2 32   40   48   ▢   ▢   ▢

Multiply.

3 6 × 8 = ▢

4 7 × 8 = ▢

5 9 × 8 = ▢

6 10 × 8 = ▢

ON YOUR OWN

**Go to Workbook A:
Practice 4, pages 105–108**

6.5 Multiply by 9

Lesson Objectives

- Understand multiplication by using array models and area models.
- Practice multiplication facts of 9.

Learn Use array models to show multiplication facts.

Serena bundles 9 straws into one group.
She bundles 3 groups of straws.
How many straws does she have in all?

Look at the array models.

1 2 3 4 5 6 7 8 9

1
2
3

3 groups of 9 straws
= 3 × 9

1 2 3

1
2
3
4
5
6
7
8
9

3 × 9 = 9 × 3
I can also show the array
as 9 × 3.

9 × 3 = 27
So, 3 × 9 = 27.
She has 27 straws in all.

Guided Learning

Look at the array model. Then express as a multiplication fact.

1

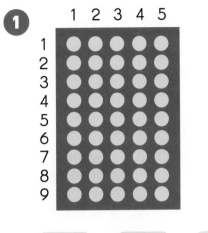

$$\boxed{} \times \boxed{} = \boxed{}$$

Show 5 × 9 on the array model. Then express as a multiplication fact.

2

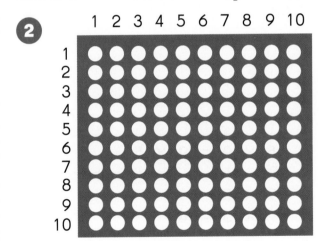

$$\boxed{} \times \boxed{} = \boxed{}$$

Learn **Use area models and multiplication facts you know to find other multiplication facts.**

4 × 9 = ?
4 × 9 = 9 × 4

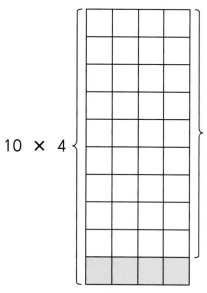

10 × 4 { 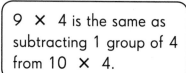 } 9 × 4

4 × 9 = 9 × 4
I can show the area model as 9 × 4.
9 × 4 = 36

9 × 4 is the same as subtracting 1 group of 4 from 10 × 4.

9 × 4 = 10 groups of 4 − 1 group of 4
      = 40 − 4
      = 36

So, 4 × 9 = 36.

. . . .

5 × 9 = ?
5 × 9 = 9 × 5

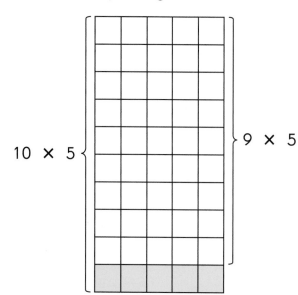

10 × 5 { } 9 × 5

5 × 9 = 9 × 5
I can show the area model as 9 × 5.
9 × 5 = 45

$9 \times 5 = 10$ groups of $5 - 1$ group of 5

$ = 50 - 5$

$ = 45$

So, $5 \times 9 = 45$.

Do you see a pattern?

9 times any number is 10 times the number minus the number.

Guided Learning

Solve. Use the area model to help you.

3 $6 \times 9 = ?$

$6 \times 9 = 9 \times 6$

$9 \times 6 = 10$ groups of $6 - \boxed{}$ group of 6

$ = 60 - \boxed{}$

$ = \boxed{}$

So, $6 \times 9 = \boxed{}$.

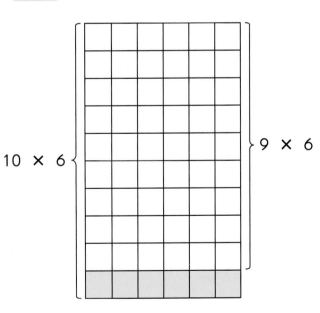

10×6

9×6

Solve. Use the area model to help you.

4 Mr. Leeson has 8 mirrors.
Each mirror has 9 sides.
How many sides do the mirrors have in all?

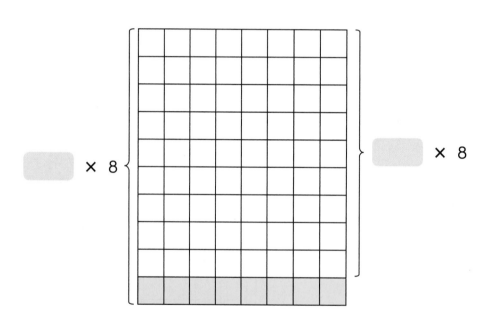

$\boxed{} \times 8$

$\boxed{} \times 8$

8 × 9 = 9 × 8

9 × 8 = 10 groups of 8 − $\boxed{}$ group of 8

$ = 80 - \boxed{}$

$ = \boxed{}$

8 mirrors have $\boxed{}$ sides in all.

Use finger counting to show multiplication facts of 9.

$1 \times 9 = 9$

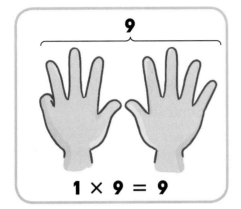

9

$1 \times 9 = 9$

$2 \times 9 = 18$

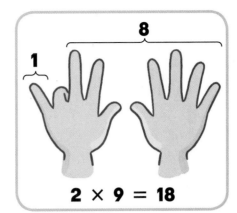

8

1

$2 \times 9 = 18$

$3 \times 9 = 27$

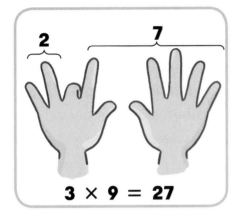

2

7

$3 \times 9 = 27$

I bend my third finger to show 3 times 9.
$3 \times 9 = 27$

Guided Learning

Multiply. Use finger counting.

5 $5 \times 9 = $ ▢

6 $9 \times 9 = $ ▢

Get to the Top!

Players: 4
Materials:
- question cards with multiplication facts of 6, 7, 8, and 9
- number board
- 8 counters for each player

Each player chooses one path on the number board.

STEP 1 Each player places a counter on the first empty space of his or her path.

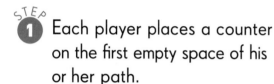

STEP 2 Player 1 draws a question card and answers the question.
For example, $5 \times 6 = 30$. The other players check the answer.

STEP 3 Player 1 places a counter on the answer if it is on his or her path.

If the answer is not on Player 1's path or if the answer is wrong, Player 1 does not place any counter on the number board.

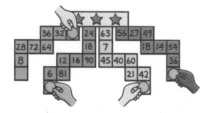

STEP 4 Players take turns. Players do not return the cards to the stack after each play.

The first player to reach the top by completely covering the path with counters wins!

Multiplication Table of 9

1	×	9	=	9
2	×	9	=	18
3	×	9	=	27
4	×	9	=	36
5	×	9	=	45
6	×	9	=	54
7	×	9	=	63
8	×	9	=	72
9	×	9	=	81
10	×	9	=	90

Let's Practice

Complete each skip-counting pattern.

1 9 18 27 ⬜ ⬜ ⬜

2 36 45 54 ⬜ ⬜ ⬜

Multiply. Use any method.

3 2 × 9 = ⬜

4 7 × 9 = ⬜

5 5 × 9 = ⬜

6 4 × 9 = ⬜

7 6 × 9 = ⬜

8 3 × 9 = ⬜

ON YOUR OWN

**Go to Workbook A:
Practice 5, pages 109–112**

Lesson 6.6 Division: Finding the Number of Items in Each Group

Lesson Objectives

- Divide to find the number of items in each group.
- Understand related multiplication and division facts.
- Write division sentences for real-world problems.

> **Vocabulary**
> equal groups

Learn Divide to find the number of items in each group by using related multiplication facts.

Divide 42 cubes into 6 **equal groups**.
How many cubes does each group have?

> Think of a related multiplication fact.

6 × 7 = 42
So, 42 ÷ 6 = 7.

Each group has 7 cubes.

Guided Learning

Solve. Use related multiplication facts to help you.

1 Divide 48 marbles into 8 equal groups.
   How many marbles does each group have?

   $8 \times 6 = 48$

   So, $48 \div 8 = $ ☐.

   Each group has ☐ marbles.

Think of a related multiplication fact.

2 Divide 35 glasses equally among 7 trays.
   How many glasses does each tray have? ☐

Let's Practice

Find the missing numbers.

1 $8 \times$ ☐ $= 56$ So, $56 \div 8 = $ ☐.

2 $7 \times$ ☐ $= 49$ So, $49 \div 7 = $ ☐.

Express two division sentences for each multiplication sentence.

3 $9 \times 4 = 36$ ☐

4 $5 \times 7 = 35$ ☐

Solve. Use related multiplication facts to help you.

5 Divide 48 beads into 8 equal containers.
   How many beads does each container have? ☐

ON YOUR OWN

Go to Workbook A:
Practice 6, pages 113–114

6.7 Division: Making Equal Groups

Lesson Objectives

- Divide to find the number of groups.
- Understand related multiplication and division facts.
- Express division sentences for real-world problems.

Learn **Divide to make equal groups by using related multiplication facts.**

Divide 56 stars into equal groups.
Each group has 8 stars.
How many groups are formed?

Think of a related multiplication fact.

7 × 8 = 56
So, 56 ÷ 8 = 7.
7 groups are formed.

Guided Learning

Solve. Use related multiplication facts to help you.

1 Divide 54 crackers into equal plates of 6 crackers.
How many plates are needed?

[　　] × 6 = 54

So, 54 ÷ 6 = [　　].

[　　] plates are needed.

Think of a related multiplication fact.

2 Jim packs 63 pencils into some boxes equally.
Each box contains 9 pencils.
How many boxes does Jim use? [　　]

 Hands-On Activity

WORK IN PAIRS

Tell a division story by arranging objects into groups of 6, 7, 8, or 9.
Have a classmate solve it.

Example

Benny has to store 36 stuffed animals in boxes.
He puts 9 stuffed animals in each box.

How many boxes does Benny use?

36 ÷ 9 = 4

Benny uses 4 boxes.

Let's Practice

Find the missing numbers.

1 ☐ × 7 = 28

So, 28 ÷ 7 = ☐ .

2 ☐ × 8 = 48

So, 48 ÷ 8 = ☐ .

Express two division sentences for each multiplication sentence.

3 6 × 9 = ☐

4 7 × 6 = ☐

Divide. Use related multiplication facts to help you.

5 36 ÷ 6 = ☐

6 63 ÷ 7 = ☐

7 40 ÷ 8 = ☐

8 72 ÷ 9 = ☐

Solve. Use related multiplication facts to help you.

9 Betty puts 9 raisins in a muffin.
She uses 45 raisins in all.
How many muffins does she puts raisins in? ☐

10 Shona collects 32 leaves.
She pastes 8 leaves on each page of her scrapbook.
How many pages of her scrapbook does she fill? ☐

ON YOUR OWN

Go to Workbook A:
Practice 7, page 115

Put On Your Thinking Cap!

PROBLEM SOLVING

Find the numbers.

Example

I have a number.
When I multiply the number by 9, the answer is 72.
What is my number?

I divide 72 by 9.
$72 \div 9 = 8$

My number is 8.

I can work backward to find the answer.

I divide because it is the opposite of multiplying.

1 I have two numbers.
When I multiply each number by 8, the answers will both be less than 60 but greater than 45.
What are my numbers?

2 Make up your own multiplication or division riddle and have a classmate solve it.

ON YOUR OWN

**Go to Workbook A:
Put On Your Thinking Cap!
pages 117–118**

Chapter Wrap Up

Study Guide
You have learned...

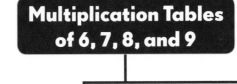

Multiplication Tables of 6, 7, 8, and 9

Multiplication Properties

Commutative Property

Changing the order of numbers in a multiplication sentence does not change the answer.

Example

4 × 5 = 20
5 × 4 = 20

So, 4 × 5 = 5 × 4
        = 20.

Multiplicative Property of One

Any number multiplied by 1 equals that number.

Example

1 × 6 = 6
6 × 1 = 6

1 × 9 = 9
9 × 1 = 9

Multiplicative Property of Zero

Any number multiplied by equals 0.

Example

5 × 0 = 0
0 × 5 = 0

8 × 0 = 0
0 × 8 = 0

Associative Property

Changing the way numbers in a multiplication sentence are grouped and multiplied does not change the answer

Example

2 × 3 × 3 = **6** × 3
          = 18
2 × **3 × 3** = 2 × **9**
          = **18**

In both methods, you get the same answer.

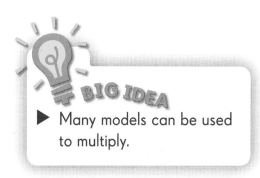
Multiplication Model

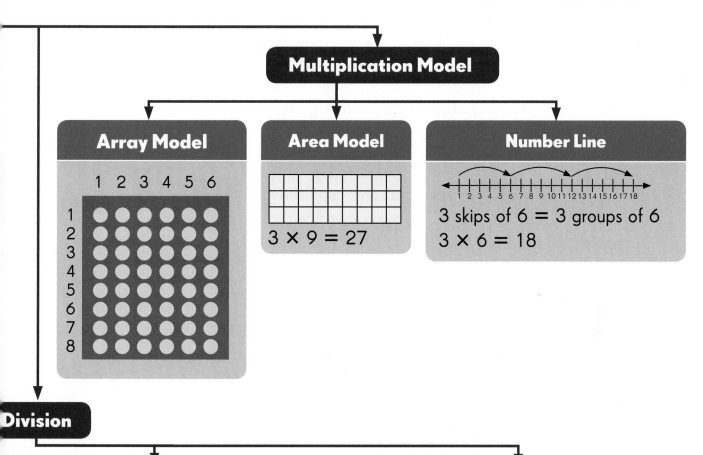

Array Model

1 2 3 4 5 6
1
2
3
4
5
6
7
8

Area Model

$3 \times 9 = 27$

Number Line

1 2 3 4 5 6 7 8 9 10 11 12 13 14 15 16 17 18

3 skips of 6 = 3 groups of 6
$3 \times 6 = 18$

Division

Dividing to Find the Number of Items in Each Group

ulie divides 56 flowers equally in 7 vases.
How many flowers does each vase hold?

$7 \times 8 = 56$

$56 \div 7 = 8$

Each vase holds 8 flowers.

Dividing to Make Equal Groups

Abel divides 36 footballs into equal groups.
There are 9 footballs in each group.
How many groups of football does
Abel form?

$4 \times 9 = 36$

$36 \div 9 = 4$

Abel forms 4 groups of footballs.

Chapter Review/Test

Vocabulary

Choose the correct word.

 When using a number line to multiply, the number of ___ shows the number of equal groups.

2 When items are divided into ___ groups, the number of items in each group is the same.

3 The ___ property states that changing the order of numbers in a multiplication sentence does not change the answer.

4 The ___ property states that changing the way numbers in a multiplication sentence are grouped and multiplied does not change the answer.

| commutative |
| associative |
| array |
| division |
| skips |
| equal |

Concepts and Skills

Find the array model that shows 2 × 5.

a

b

c

Find the missing number. Choose the correct area model.

6 7 × 9 = [ ]

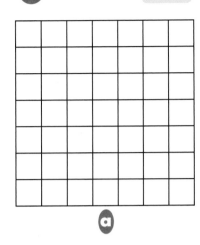

ⓐ

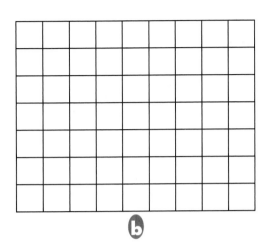

ⓑ

Express the multiplication fact in Exercise 6 another way. Choose the correct area model.

7 [ ] × [ ] = [ ]

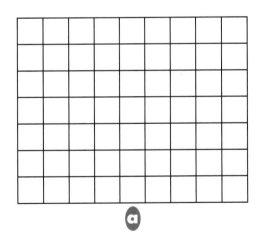

ⓐ

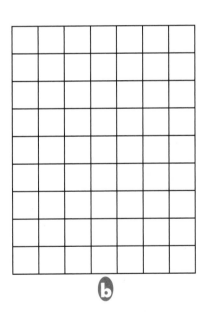

ⓑ

Look at the number line. Then express as a multiplication fact.

8

[ ] × [ ] = [ ]

Express the multiplication sentence in Exercise 8 in another way. Use the number line provided.

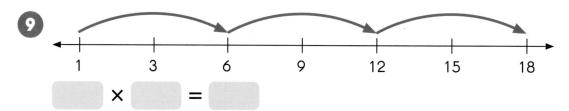

⑨

$$\boxed{} \times \boxed{} = \boxed{}$$

Multiply.

⑩ $2 \times 6 = \boxed{}$

⑪ $3 \times 7 = \boxed{}$

⑫ $5 \times 9 = \boxed{}$

⑬ $5 \times 8 = \boxed{}$

⑭ $6 \times 7 = \boxed{}$

⑮ $8 \times 1 = \boxed{}$

⑯ $0 \times 5 = \boxed{}$

⑰ $10 \times 9 = \boxed{}$

Find the missing numbers.

⑱ $5 \times 1 \times 9 = \boxed{} \times 9$

$= \boxed{}$

⑲ $8 \times 5 \times 2 = 8 \times \boxed{}$

$= \boxed{}$

⑳ $5 \times 6 = \boxed{}$

$\boxed{} \div 6 = 5$

㉑ $7 \times \boxed{} = 28$

$28 \div 7 = \boxed{}$

㉒ $\boxed{} \times 9 = 72$

$72 \div 9 = \boxed{}$

㉓ $80 \div \boxed{} = 8$

$\boxed{} \times 8 = 80$

Problem Solving

Solve.

㉔ Mr. Johnson owns 7 cats. Each cat has 6 kittens. How many kittens does Mr. Johnson own? $\boxed{}$

㉕ Martin has 81 sheep. He divides his sheep equally into 9 pens. How many sheep are put in each pen? $\boxed{}$

㉖ Ellen has 63 cherries. She puts 7 cherries into each bowl. How many bowls does she use? $\boxed{}$

7 Multiplication

Let's Have Fun With Spiders!

Ingredients:
pretzel
crackers
honey
raisins

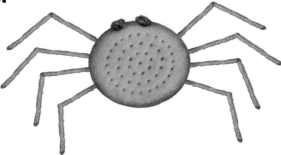

Body: Use crackers.

Legs: Use eight 6-centimeter pieces of pretzel. Stick four pieces to each side of the crackers with honey.

Eyes: Use two small raisins. Stick each of them on top of the cracker with honey.

Break each pretzel to make the legs look jointed.

How many legs does a spider have? I want to make 5 spiders. How many pieces of pretzel do I need for the legs?

Lessons
7.1 Mental Multiplication
7.2 Multiplying Without Regrouping
7.3 Multiplying Ones, Tens, and Hundreds with Regrouping

BIG IDEAS

▶ Mental math can be used to multiply.
▶ Numbers up to 3-digits can be multiplied with or without regrouping.

Recall Prior Knowledge

Multiplication as repeated addition

$7 + 7 + 7 + 7 + 7 + 7 = 42$
$6 \times 7 = 42$

$10 + 10 + 10 = 30$
$3 \times 10 = 30$

Multiplication as skip counting

Skip-counting by 3

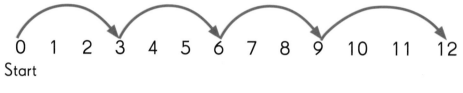

0   1   2   3   4   5   6   7   8   9   10   11   12
Start

$4 \times 3 = 12$

Multiplication tables of 2, 3, 4, and 5

$1 \times 2 = 2$	$1 \times 3 = 3$	$1 \times 4 = 4$	$1 \times 5 = 5$
$2 \times 2 = 4$	$2 \times 3 = 6$	$2 \times 4 = 8$	$2 \times 5 = 10$
$3 \times 2 = 6$	$3 \times 3 = 9$	$3 \times 4 = 12$	$3 \times 5 = 15$
$4 \times 2 = 8$	$4 \times 3 = 12$	$4 \times 4 = 16$	$4 \times 5 = 20$
$5 \times 2 = 10$	$5 \times 3 = 15$	$5 \times 4 = 20$	$5 \times 5 = 25$
$6 \times 2 = 12$	$6 \times 3 = 18$	$6 \times 4 = 24$	$6 \times 5 = 30$
$7 \times 2 = 14$	$7 \times 3 = 21$	$7 \times 4 = 28$	$7 \times 5 = 35$
$8 \times 2 = 16$	$8 \times 3 = 24$	$8 \times 4 = 32$	$8 \times 5 = 40$
$9 \times 2 = 18$	$9 \times 3 = 27$	$9 \times 4 = 36$	$9 \times 5 = 45$
$10 \times 2 = 20$	$10 \times 3 = 30$	$10 \times 4 = 40$	$10 \times 5 = 50$

Multiplication tables of 6, 7, 8, 9, and 10

1 × 6 = 6	1 × 7 = 7	1 × 8 = 8	1 × 9 = 9	1 × 10 = 10
2 × 6 = 12	2 × 7 = 14	2 × 8 = 16	2 × 9 = 18	2 × 10 = 20
3 × 6 = 18	3 × 7 = 21	3 × 8 = 24	3 × 9 = 27	3 × 10 = 30
4 × 6 = 24	4 × 7 = 28	4 × 8 = 32	4 × 9 = 36	4 × 10 = 40
5 × 6 = 30	5 × 7 = 35	5 × 8 = 40	5 × 9 = 45	5 × 10 = 50
6 × 6 = 36	6 × 7 = 42	6 × 8 = 48	6 × 9 = 54	6 × 10 = 60
7 × 6 = 42	7 × 7 = 49	7 × 8 = 56	7 × 9 = 63	7 × 10 = 70
8 × 6 = 48	8 × 7 = 56	8 × 8 = 64	8 × 9 = 72	8 × 10 = 80
9 × 6 = 54	9 × 7 = 63	9 × 8 = 72	9 × 9 = 81	9 × 10 = 90
10 × 6 = 60	10 × 7 = 70	10 × 8 = 80	10 × 9 = 90	10 × 10 = 100

Multiplying numbers in any order

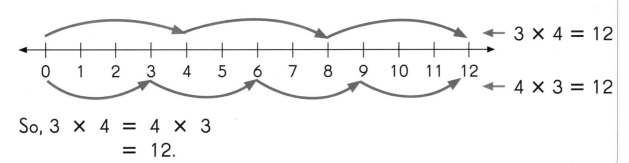

$3 \times 4 = 12$

$4 \times 3 = 12$

So, $3 \times 4 = 4 \times 3$
$= 12.$

Using multiplication facts you know to find other multiplication facts

$6 \times 7 = 5$ groups of $7 + 1$ group of 7
$= 35 + 7$
$= 42$

$9 \times 7 = 10$ groups of $7 - 1$ group of 7
$= 70 - 7$
$= 63$

Recall Prior Knowledge

Multiplying by 0

Any number multiplied by 0 equals 0.
$0 \times 10 = 0$
$4 \times 0 = 0$

Multiplying by 1

Any number multiplied by 1 equals that number.
$1 \times 3 = 3$ $7 \times 1 = 7$

✔ Quick Check

Find the missing numbers.

1 $4 + 4 + 4 + 4 + 4 = \boxed{} \times 4$

$ = \boxed{}$

2

5   10 $\boxed{}$ $\boxed{}$ 25   30   35   40 $\boxed{}$ $\boxed{}$

Find the missing numbers.

3 $7 \times 5 = \boxed{}$

So, $5 \times 7 = \boxed{}$.

Find the missing numbers.

4 $7 \times 8 = 5$ groups of $8 + \boxed{}$ groups of 8

$ = 40 + \boxed{}$

$ = \boxed{}$

5 $8 \times 6 = 10$ groups of $6 - \boxed{}$ groups of 6

$ = 60 - \boxed{}$

$ = \boxed{}$

Multiply.

6 $7 \times 9 = \boxed{}$ **7** $7 \times 7 = \boxed{}$ **8** $9 \times 6 = \boxed{}$

7.1 Mental Multiplication

Lesson Objective

- Multiply ones, tens, and hundreds mentally.

Learn — Multiply ones mentally.

Find 4 × 3.

4 × 3 = 12

Find 3 × 4.

3 × 4 = 12

I skip-count by 3s.
  3 6 9 12
I skip-count by 4s.
  4   8   12
So, 4 × 3 is the same as 3 × 4.

Guided Learning

Multiply. Find the missing numbers.

1 4 × 6 = ?

6 × 4 = [ ]

4 × 6 = [ ]

2 8 × 3 = ?

3 × 8 = [ ]

8 × 3 = [ ]

3 5 × 7 = ?

7 × 5 = [ ]

5 × 7 = [ ]

4 9 × 10 = ?

10 × 9 = [ ]

9 × 10 = [ ]

Multiply by tens or hundreds mentally.

Find 5 × 40.
Find 5 × 400.

5 × 4 = 20

5 × 40 = 5 × 4 tens
       = 20 tens
       = 200
So, 5 × 40 = 200.

5 × 400 = 5 × 4 hundreds
        = 20 hundreds
        = 2,000
So, 5 × 400 = 2,000.

×	4	40	400
5	20	200	2,000

Do you see a pattern?

Guided Learning

Multiply. Find the missing numbers.

5 Find 6 × 70.

6 × 70 = 6 × [ ] tens

     = [ ] tens

     = [ ]

So, 6 × 70 = [ ].

6 Find 6 × 700.

6 × 700 = 6 × [ ] hundreds

     = [ ] hundreds

     = [ ]

So, 6 × 700 = [ ].

Multiply. Use mental math.

7 8 × 60 = [ ]

8 9 × 400 = [ ]

8 × 6 = [ ]
So, 8 × 60 = [ ].

9 × 4 = [ ]
So, 9 × 400 = [ ].

9 7 × 50 = [ ]

10 90 × 6 = [ ]

11 5 × 70 = [ ]

12 8 × 100 = [ ]

13 600 × 4 = [ ]

14 9 × 800 = [ ]

Let's Practice

Multiply. Use mental math.

1 7 × 6 = [ ]

2 9 × 8 = [ ]

3 4 × 80 = [ ]

4 70 × 3 = [ ]

5 6 × 40 = [ ]

6 20 × 9 = [ ]

7 8 × 700 = [ ]

8 900 × 5 = [ ]

9 7 × 600 = [ ]

10 400 × 2 = [ ]

Recall
4 × 8
7 × 3
6 × 4
2 × 9
8 × 7
9 × 5
7 × 6
4 × 2

ON YOUR OWN

Go to Workbook A:
Practice 1, pages 119–120

7.2 Multiplying Without Regrouping

Lesson Objective

- Multiply ones, tens, and hundreds without regrouping.

Vocabulary
product

Learn **Multiply a 2-digit number without regrouping using base-ten blocks.**

$3 \times 12 = ?$

Tens	Ones
	🔲 🔲
	🔲 🔲
	🔲 🔲

Step 1
Multiply the **ones** by 3.

$$\begin{array}{r} 1\ 2 \\ \times\ \ \ 3 \\ \hline \mathbf{6} \end{array}$$

3×2 ones $= 6$ ones

Tens	Ones
▨	🔲 🔲
▨	🔲 🔲
▨	🔲 🔲
$3 \times 10 = 30$	$3 \times 2 = 6$

Step 2
Multiply the **tens** by 3.

$$\begin{array}{r} 1\ 2 \\ \times\ \ \ 3 \\ \hline \mathbf{3}\ 6 \end{array}$$

3×1 ten $= 3$ tens

So, $3 \times 12 = 36$.

36 is the **product** of 3 and 12.

Multiply a 3-digit number without regrouping using base-ten blocks.

$2 \times 341 = ?$

Hundreds	Tens	Ones
		⬜
		⬜

Step 1
Multiply the **ones** by 2.

$$\begin{array}{r} 3\ 4\ 1 \\ \times\quad 2 \\ \hline \mathbf{2} \end{array}$$

2×1 one $= 2$ ones

Hundreds	Tens	Ones
	▦▦▦▦	⬜
	▦▦▦▦	⬜

Step 2
Multiply the **tens** by 2.

$$\begin{array}{r} 3\ 4\ 1 \\ \times\quad 2 \\ \hline \mathbf{8}\ 2 \end{array}$$

2×4 tens $= 8$ tens

Hundreds	Tens	Ones
▦▦▦	▦▦▦▦	⬜
▦▦▦	▦▦▦▦	⬜
$2 \times 300 = 600$	$2 \times 40 = 80$	$2 \times 1 = 2$

Step 3
Multiply the **hundreds** by 2.

$$\begin{array}{r} 3\ 4\ 1 \\ \times\quad 2 \\ \hline \mathbf{6}\ 8\ 2 \end{array}$$

2×3 hundreds $= 6$ hundreds

So, $2 \times 341 = 682$.

682 is the product of 2 and 341.

Guided Learning

Find the missing numbers.

1 2 × 34 = ?

Step 1 Multiply the ones by 2.

2 × 4 ones = [ ] ones

```
    3 4
  ×   2
  ─────
  [   ]
```

Step 2 Multiply the tens by 2.

2 × 3 tens = [ ] tens

So, 2 × 34 = [ ] .

```
    3 4
  ×   2
  ─────
  [ ] [ ]
```

2 3 × 132 = ?

Step 1 Multiply the ones by 3.

3 × [ ] ones = [ ] ones

```
  1 3 2
  ×   3
  ─────
    [ ]
```

Step 2 Multiply the tens by 3.

3 × [ ] tens = [ ] tens

```
  1 3 2
  ×   3
  ─────
  [ ] [ ]
```

Step 3 Multiply the hundreds by 3.

3 × [ ] hundred = [ ] hundreds

So, 3 × 132 = [ ] .

```
  1 3 2
  ×   3
  ─────
  [ ] [ ] [ ]
```

Multiply.

3
```
    2 4
  ×   2
  ─────
  [     ]
```

4
```
    4 0
  ×   2
  ─────
  [     ]
```

5
```
    2 3 2
  ×     3
  ─────
  [     ]
```

6
```
    1 1 2
  ×     4
  ─────
  [     ]
```

Hands-On Activity

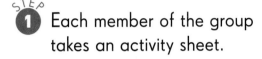

WORKING TOGETHER

Players: 3
Materials:
• activity sheets A to F
• multiplier cards
with numbers 2, 3, and 4

STEP 1 Each member of the group takes an activity sheet.

Activity Sheet A

H	T	O	
2	2	1	
x			

STEP 2 Group member selects a multiplier card.

STEP 3 Group member places the multiplier card on the ones place on his or her activity sheet. Then he or she finds the product of the number on the activity sheet and the number on the card. The other group members check the answer.

Activity Sheet A

H	T	O	
2	2	1	
x		3	

STEP 4 The group members take turns to complete their worksheets. Each player completes 2 worksheets.

Let's Practice

Find the missing numbers.

1 3 × 32 = ?

3 × 2 ones = ⬚ ones

3 × 3 tens = ⬚ tens

So, 3 × 32 = ⬚ .

Multiply the ones.
Then multiply the tens.

2 2 × 214 = ?

2 × ⬚ ones = ⬚ ones

2 × ⬚ ten = ⬚ tens

2 × ⬚ hundreds = ⬚ hundreds

So, 2 × 214 = ⬚ .

Multiply the ones.
Then multiply the
tens, followed by
the hundreds.

Multiply.

3
```
   2 3
 ×   2
 ⬚⬚⬚
```

4
```
   1 1
 ×   3
 ⬚⬚⬚
```

5
```
   4 2 1
 ×     2
  ⬚⬚⬚
```

6
```
   2 1 3
 ×     3
  ⬚⬚⬚
```

ON YOUR OWN

Go to Workbook A:
Practice 2, page 121–126

7.3 Multiplying Ones, Tens, and Hundreds with Regrouping

Lesson Objective

- Multiply ones, tens, and hundreds with regrouping.

Learn **Multiply a 2-digit number with regrouping of ones.**

$5 \times 15 = ?$

Hundreds	Tens	Ones
		•••••

Step 1
Multiply the **ones** by 5.

$$\begin{array}{r} \overset{2}{1}\,5 \\ \times \quad 5 \\ \hline \mathbf{5} \end{array}$$

5×5 ones $= 25$ ones

Hundreds	Tens	Ones
	▨▨	•••••

Regroup the ones.
25 ones $=$ 2 tens 5 ones

Hundreds	Tens	Ones
	▨▨▨▨▨▨▨	•••••

Step 2
Multiply the **tens** by 5.

$$\begin{array}{r} \overset{2}{1}\,5 \\ \times \quad 5 \\ \hline \mathbf{7}\,5 \end{array}$$

5×1 ten $= 5$ tens

Add the tens.
2 tens $+$ 5 tens $=$ 7 tens

So, $5 \times 15 = 75$.

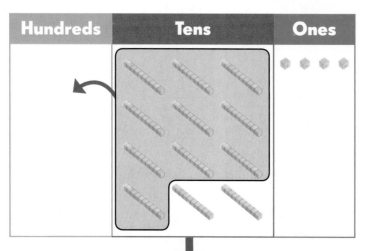

Multiply a 2-digit number with regrouping of tens.

$4 \times 31 = ?$

Hundreds	Tens	Ones
		▪ ▪ ▪ ▪

Step 1
Multiply the **ones** by 4.

$$\begin{array}{r} 3\ 1 \\ \times\quad 4 \\ \hline \mathbf{4} \end{array}$$

4×1 one $= 4$ ones

Hundreds	Tens	Ones
		▪ ▪ ▪ ▪

Step 2
Multiply the **tens** by 4.

$$\begin{array}{r} 3\ 1 \\ \times\quad 4 \\ \hline \mathbf{12}\,4 \end{array}$$

4×3 tens $= 12$ tens

Hundreds	Tens	Ones
		▪ ▪ ▪ ▪

Regroup the tens.
12 tens = 1 hundred 2 tens

So, $4 \times 31 = 124$.

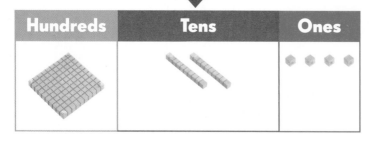

Guided Learning

Find the missing numbers.

1 5 × 12 = ?

Step 1 Multiply the ones by 5.

5 × [ ] ones = [ ] ones

Regroup the ones.

[ ] ones = [ ] ten [ ] ones

```
      [ ]
      1 2
  ×     5
      [ ]
```

Step 2 Multiply the tens by 5.

5 × [ ] ten = [ ] tens

Add the tens.

[ ] ten + [ ] tens = [ ] tens.

So, 5 × 12 = [ ].

```
      [ ]
      1 2
  ×     5
      [ ]
```

2
```
    2 3
  ×   4
  [ ]
```

3
```
    4 9
  ×   2
  [ ]
```

4
```
    1 7
  ×   3
  [ ]
```

Find the missing numbers.

5 40 × 3 = ?

Step 1 Multiply the ones by 3.

3 × [ ] ones = [ ] ones

```
    4 0
  ×   3
  [ ]
```

Step 2 Multiply the tens by 3.

3 × [ ] tens = [ ] tens

Regroup the tens.

[ ] tens = [ ] hundred [ ] tens

```
    4 0
  ×   3
  [ ]
```

So, 40 × 3 = [ ].

6
$$\begin{array}{r} 37 \\ \times\ \ 3 \\ \hline \end{array}$$

7
$$\begin{array}{r} 60 \\ \times\ \ 5 \\ \hline \end{array}$$

8
$$\begin{array}{r} 81 \\ \times\ \ 4 \\ \hline \end{array}$$

Learn **Multiply a 2-digit number with regrouping of ones and tens.**

$2 \times 68 = ?$

Hundreds	Tens	Ones
		••••• •••
		[●●●●●●●●]

Step 1
Multiply the **ones** by 2.

$$\begin{array}{r} \overset{1}{6}\,8 \\ \times\ \ \ 2 \\ \hline 6 \end{array}$$

2×8 ones $= 16$ ones

Hundreds	Tens	Ones
	|	●●●● ●●

Regroup the ones.
16 ones = 1 ten 6 ones

Hundreds	Tens	Ones
		●●●● ●●

Step 2
Multiply the **tens** by 2.

$$\begin{array}{r} \overset{1}{6}\,8 \\ \times\ \ \ 2 \\ \hline \mathbf{13}6 \end{array}$$

2×6 tens $= 12$ tens

Add the tens.
1 ten + 12 tens = 13 tens

Hundreds	Tens	Ones
[flat]	|||	●●●● ●●

Regroup the tens.
13 tens = 1 hundred 3 tens

So, $2 \times 68 = 136$.

Guided Learning

Find the missing numbers.

9 2 × 69 = ?

Step 1 Multiply the ones by 2.

2 × 9 ones = [ ] ones

Regroup the ones.

[ ] ones = [ ] ten [ ] ones

[ ]
69
× 2
[ ]

Step 2 Multiply the tens by 2.

2 × 6 tens = [ ] tens

Add the tens.

[ ] ten + [ ] tens = [ ] tens

Regroup the tens.

[ ] tens = [ ] hundred [ ] tens

So, 2 × 69 = [ ].

[ ]
69
× 2
[ ]

Multiply.

10
```
   9 3
×    5
```
[ ]

11
```
   2 4
×    5
```
[ ]

12
```
   7 6
×    2
```
[ ]

13
```
   8 8
×    2
```
[ ]

14
```
   5 8
×    4
```
[ ]

15
```
   4 8
×    3
```
[ ]

Multiply a 3-digit number with regrouping of ones, tens, and hundreds.

5 × 146 = ?

Hundreds	Tens	Ones
		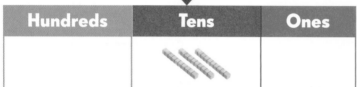

Step 1
Multiply the **ones** by 5.

$$\begin{array}{r} \overset{3}{}146 \\ \times5 \\ \hline 0 \end{array}$$

5 × 6 ones = 30 ones

Hundreds	Tens	Ones

Regroup the ones.
30 ones = 3 tens 0 ones

Hundreds	Tens	Ones

Step 2
Multiply the **tens** by 5.

$$\begin{array}{r} \overset{2}{}\overset{3}{1}46 \\ \times5 \\ \hline 30 \end{array}$$

5 × 4 tens = 20 tens

Add the tens.
3 tens + 20 tens = 23 tens

Hundreds	Tens	Ones
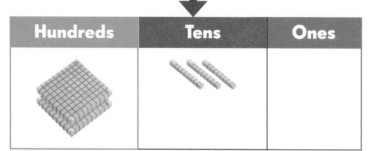		

Regroup the tens.
23 tens = 2 hundreds 3 tens

Hundreds	Tens	Ones

Step 3
Multiply the **hundreds** by 5.

$$\begin{array}{r} \overset{2\ 3}{1\ 4\ 6} \\ \times\ \ \ \ 5 \\ \hline \mathbf{7}3\ 0 \end{array}$$

5 × 1 hundred = 5 hundreds

Add the hundreds.

2 hundreds + 5 hundreds
= 7 hundreds

So, 5 × 146 = 730.

Guided Learning

Find the missing numbers.

16 4 × 157 = ?

Step 1 Multiply the ones by 4.

4 × ⬜ ones = ⬜ ones

Regroup the ones.

⬜ ones = ⬜ tens ⬜ ones

$$\begin{array}{r} \square \\ 1\ 5\ 7 \\ \times\ \ \ \ 4 \\ \hline \square \end{array}$$

Step 2 Multiply the tens by 4.

4 × ⬜ tens = ⬜ tens

Add the tens.

⬜ tens + ⬜ tens = ⬜ tens

Regroup the tens.

⬜ tens = ⬜ hundreds ⬜ tens

$$\begin{array}{r} 1\ 5\ 7 \\ \times\ \ \ \ 4 \\ \hline \square \end{array}$$

Step 3 Multiply the hundreds by 4.

4 × ▢ hundred = ▢ hundreds

$$\begin{array}{r} 1\ 5\ 7 \\ \times \quad 4 \\ \hline \end{array}$$

Add the hundreds.

▢ hundreds + ▢ hundreds = ▢ hundreds

So, 4 × 157 = ▢.

Multiply.

17
$$\begin{array}{r} 3\ 9\ 5 \\ \times \quad 2 \\ \hline \end{array}$$

18
$$\begin{array}{r} 2\ 7\ 8 \\ \times \quad 3 \\ \hline \end{array}$$

19
$$\begin{array}{r} 1\ 6\ 8 \\ \times \quad 5 \\ \hline \end{array}$$

20
$$\begin{array}{r} 2\ 4\ 7 \\ \times \quad 4 \\ \hline \end{array}$$

21
$$\begin{array}{r} 1\ 7\ 0 \\ \times \quad 3 \\ \hline \end{array}$$

22
$$\begin{array}{r} 3\ 6\ 9 \\ \times \quad 2 \\ \hline \end{array}$$

Spin and Multiply!

Players: **2 to 4**
Materials:
- transparent spinner base
- 1 spinner with numbers 2, 3, 4, and 5
- game cards 1 to 4

 STEP 1 Player 1 picks a game card.

 STEP 2 Player 1 turns the spinner to get a number.

STEP 3 Player 1 writes the number in the box on the game card. He or she multiplies the numbers. The other players check the answer.

STEP 4 The players take turns finding products until each game card is full.

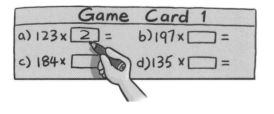

The player with the most correct answers wins!

Let's Practice

Find the missing numbers.

1 3 × 58 = ?

Step 1   Multiply the ones by 3.

3 × 8 ones = [ ] ones

Regroup the ones.

[ ] ones = [ ] tens [ ] ones

```
    [ ]
    5 8
×     3
    [ ]
```

Step 2   Multiply the tens by 3.

3 × 5 tens = [ ] tens

Add the tens.

[ ] tens + [ ] tens = [ ] tens

Regroup the tens.

[ ] tens = [ ] hundred [ ] tens

```
    [ ]
    5 8
×     3
    [ ]
```

So, 3 × 58 = [ ].

2 5 × 147 = ?

Step 1   Multiply the ones by 5.

5 × 7 ones = [ ] ones

Regroup the ones.

[ ] ones = [ ] tens [ ] ones

$$\begin{array}{r} \square \\ 1\ 4\ 7 \\ \times\ \ \ \ 5 \\ \hline \square \end{array}$$

Step 2   Multiply the tens by 5.

5 × 4 tens = [ ] tens

Add the tens.

[ ] tens + [ ] tens = [ ] tens

Regroup the tens.

[ ] tens = [ ] hundreds [ ] tens

$$\begin{array}{r} \square\ \square \\ 1\ \ 4\ 7 \\ \times\ \ \ \ \ \ 5 \\ \hline \square \end{array}$$

Step 3   Multiply the hundreds by 5.

5 × 1 hundred = [ ] hundreds

Add the hundreds.

[ ] hundreds + [ ] hundreds = [ ] hundreds

So, 5 × 147 = [ ] .

$$\begin{array}{r} \square\ \square \\ 1\ \ 4\ 7 \\ \times\ \ \ \ \ \ 5 \\ \hline \square \end{array}$$

3
$$\begin{array}{r} 2\ 4 \\ \times\ \ \ 3 \\ \hline \square \end{array}$$

4
$$\begin{array}{r} 5\ 2 \\ \times\ \ \ 4 \\ \hline \square \end{array}$$

5
$$\begin{array}{r} 5\ 5 \\ \times\ \ \ 2 \\ \hline \square \end{array}$$

6
$$\begin{array}{r} 1\ 1\ 4 \\ \times\ \ \ \ \ 5 \\ \hline \square \end{array}$$

7
$$\begin{array}{r} 2\ 8\ 2 \\ \times\ \ \ \ \ 3 \\ \hline \square \end{array}$$

8
$$\begin{array}{r} 3\ 8\ 7 \\ \times\ \ \ \ \ 2 \\ \hline \square \end{array}$$

ON YOUR OWN

Go to Workbook A:
Practice 3 and 4, pages 127–137

CRITICAL THINKING SKILLS
Put On Your Thinking Cap!

STEP 1 Here are eight number cards.

1 2 3 4 6 7 8 9

Find pairs of numbers that add to make 10.

a How many pairs of 10 do you get?

b Sum of the eight numbers = [ ] × 10

= [ ]

STEP 2 Without adding the numbers one by one, find the sum of numbers 2 to 9.

Find pairs of numbers that give the same sum.

ON YOUR OWN

**Go to Workbook A:
Put On Your Thinking Cap!
pages 139–140**

Chapter Wrap Up

Study Guide
You have learned...

BIG IDEAS

▶ Mental math can be used to multiply.
▶ Numbers up to 3-digits can be multiplied with or without regrouping.

Multiplication

Mental Multiplication Strategies	Multiplication Without Regrouping	Multiplication with Regrouping

Mental Multiplication Strategies

$4 \times 6 = 24$
So, $6 \times 4 = 24$.
4×6 is the same as 6×4.

$7 \times 30 = 7 \times 3$ tens
$\quad\quad\quad = 21$ tens
$\quad\quad\quad = 210$
So, $7 \times 30 = 210$.

$7 \times 300 = 7 \times 3$ hundreds
$\quad\quad\quad\quad = 21$ hundreds
$\quad\quad\quad\quad = 2,100$
So, $7 \times 300 = 2,100$.

Multiplication Without Regrouping

$$\begin{array}{r} 3\,4 \\ \times \quad 2 \\ \hline 6\,8 \end{array} \qquad \begin{array}{r} 2\,0\,3 \\ \times \quad\ 3 \\ \hline 6\,0\,9 \end{array}$$

Multiplication with Regrouping

$$\begin{array}{r} \overset{3}{7}\,8 \\ \times \quad 4 \\ \hline 3\,1\,2 \end{array} \qquad \begin{array}{r} \overset{1}{4}\,\overset{1}{5}\,6 \\ \times \quad\ 2 \\ \hline 9\,1\,2 \end{array}$$

Chapter Review/Test

Vocabulary
Choose the correct word.

product
regroup
multiply

1 When you ▢ 4 tens by 3, you get 12 tens.

2 When you ▢ 12 tens, you get 1 hundred and 2 tens.

3 When you multiply numbers, the answer is the ▢.

Concepts and Skills
Find the missing numbers.

4 6 × 5 = 30
So, 5 × 6 = ▢.

5 8 × 40 = 8 × ▢ tens

= ▢ tens

= ▢

6 9 × 200 = ▢ × ▢ hundreds

= ▢ hundreds

= ▢

Multiply.

7
```
   1 2
×    4
```
▢

8
```
   4 8
×    2
```
▢

9
```
   7 1
×    2
```
▢

10
```
   8 8
×    5
```
▢

11
```
   1 3 4
×      2
```
▢

12
```
   3 0 3
×      2
```
▢

13
$$\begin{array}{r} 124 \\ \times \quad 3 \\ \hline \end{array}$$

14
$$\begin{array}{r} 203 \\ \times \quad 4 \\ \hline \end{array}$$

15
$$\begin{array}{r} 83 \\ \times \quad 3 \\ \hline \end{array}$$

16
$$\begin{array}{r} 261 \\ \times \quad 3 \\ \hline \end{array}$$

17
$$\begin{array}{r} 297 \\ \times \quad 3 \\ \hline \end{array}$$

18
$$\begin{array}{r} 236 \\ \times \quad 4 \\ \hline \end{array}$$

Problem Solving

Solve.

19 Martin has 43 tricycles. How many wheels do the tricycles have in all?

20 There are 4 theaters. Each theater has 249 seats. How many seats are there in all?

8 Division

Try making 2 equal groups with:

1 6, 8, 10, 12, or 14 children.

2 5, 7, 9, 11, or 13 children.

What do you notice when you try to make 2 equal groups with odd numbers?

Lessons

8.1 Mental Division

8.2 Quotient and Remainder

8.3 Odd and Even Numbers

8.4 Division Without Remainder and Regrouping

8.5 Division with Regrouping in Tens and Ones

BIG IDEA

▶ There can be remainders when dividing to make equal groups or when sharing equally.

Recall Prior Knowledge

Dividing to share equally

Divide 12  into 3 equal groups.
How many does each group have?

$12 \div 3 = 4$
Each group has 4 cubes.

Dividing to form equal groups

Divide 12  equally so that there are 3 in each group.
How many groups are there?

$12 \div 3 = 4$
There are 4 groups.

Division as repeated subtraction

Find $10 \div 2$.

$10 \underbrace{- 2 - 2 - 2 - 2 - 2}_{} = 0$

Subtract groups of two 5 times

So, $10 \div 2 = 5$.

✔ Quick Check

Solve.

1. Divide 15 pencils into 3 equal groups.
   How many pencils does each group have?

2. Jane has 8 apples. She eats 2 apples each day.
   How many days will it take for her to eat all the apples?

Divide. Use repeated subtraction.

3. $12 \div 2 =$

Mental Division

Lesson Objectives

- Use related multiplication facts to divide.
- Use patterns to divide multiples of 10 and 100.

Learn Use related multiplication facts to divide mentally.

Find 24 ÷ 6.

4 × 6 = 24

So, 24 ÷ 6 = 4.

Think of a related multiplication fact.

Guided Learning

Divide. Use related multiplication facts to help you.

1 35 ÷ 7 = [ ]

Think of the multiplication facts for 7.

[ ] × 7 = 35

2 63 ÷ 9 = [ ]

Think of the multiplication facts for 9.

[ ] × 9 = 63

Use related multiplication facts and patterns to divide mentally.

Find 80 ÷ 4.

Find 800 ÷ 4.

÷	8	80	800
4	2	20	200

$$80 ÷ 4 = 8 \text{ tens} ÷ 4$$
$$= 2 \text{ tens}$$
$$= 20$$

So, 80 ÷ 4 = 20.

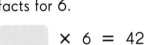

Use the multiplication facts for 4.
2 × 4 = 8
8 ÷ 4 = 2

$$800 ÷ 4 = 8 \text{ hundreds} ÷ 4$$
$$= 2 \text{ hundreds}$$
$$= 200$$

So, 800 ÷ 4 = 200.

Guided Learning

Find the missing numbers.
Use related multiplication facts and patterns to help you.

3 42 ÷ 6 = ?

420 ÷ 6 = ?

$$42 ÷ 6 = \boxed{} \text{ ones} ÷ 6$$
$$= \boxed{} \text{ ones}$$
$$= \boxed{}$$

So, 42 ÷ 6 = $\boxed{}$.

$$420 ÷ 6 = \boxed{} \text{ tens} ÷ 6$$
$$= \boxed{} \text{ tens}$$
$$= \boxed{}$$

So, 420 ÷ 6 = $\boxed{}$.

Think of the multiplication facts for 6.

$\boxed{}$ × 6 = 42

Let's Practice

Divide mentally. Use multiplication facts for 6 to help you.

1 30 ÷ 6 = [ ]   **2** 24 ÷ 6 = [ ]   **3** 54 ÷ 6 = [ ]

Divide mentally. Use multiplication facts for 7 to help you.

4 21 ÷ 7 = [ ]   **5** 42 ÷ 7 = [ ]   **6** 56 ÷ 7 = [ ]

Divide mentally. Use related multiplication facts and patterns to help you.

7 Find 300 ÷ 3.

300 ÷ 3 = [ ] hundreds ÷ 3

= [ ] hundred

= [ ]

So, 300 ÷ 3 = [ ].

8 Find 350 ÷ 5.

350 ÷ 5 = [ ] tens ÷ 5

= [ ] tens

= [ ]

So, 350 ÷ 5 = [ ].

9 700 ÷ 7 = [ ]   **10** 560 ÷ 8 = [ ]   **11** 360 ÷ 9 = [ ]

12 6,400 ÷ 8 = [ ]   **13** 7,200 ÷ 9 = [ ]   **14** 2,800 ÷ 7 = [ ]

ON YOUR OWN

Go to Workbook A:
Practice 1, pages 147–148

Lesson 8.2 Quotient and Remainder

Vocabulary
quotient
remainder

Lesson Objective

- Divide a 1-digit or a 2-digit number by a 1-digit number with or without a remainder.

Learn Divide equally.

2 children share 8 pails equally.

a How many pails does each child have?

$8 \div 2 = ?$

$$8 - 2 - 2 - 2 - 2 = 0$$
Subtract groups of two 4 times.

8 ones $\div$ 2 = 4 ones with no ones left over
Quotient   = 4 ones
$8 \div 2 = 4$

b Each child has 4 pails.

How many pails are left over?

There are no pails left over.

$2 \times \mathbf{4} = 8$

A **quotient** is the answer to a division problem.
In the division fact $8 \div 2 = 4$, the quotient is 4.

Divide with remainder.

4 children share 11 seashells equally.

ⓐ How many seashells does each child have?

11 ÷ 4 = ?

11 ones ÷ 4 = 2 ones with 3 ones
left over

= 2 R 3

Quotient = 2 ones
Remainder = 3 ones
11 ÷ 4 = 2 R 3

Each child has 2 seashells.

> Divide the 11 seashells into 4 equal groups.

> 4 × **2** = 8
> 8 is less than 11.
> 4 × **3** = 12
> 12 is more than 11.
> Choose 2 as the quotient.

ⓑ How many seashells are left over?

3 seashells are left over.

> 11 ÷ 4 = 2 R 3
> R 3 means there are 3 seashells left over. It also means that there is a remainder of 3 seashells.

A **remainder** is the number left over from a division problem.

Guided Learning

Solve.

1 3 friends share 17 starfish equally.

a How many starfish does each friend have?

17 ÷ 3 = ?

17 − ⬚ − ⬚ − ⬚ = ⬚

Subtract groups of ⬚ 3 times.

⬚ starfish are left over.

3 × **5** = 15
15 is less than 17.
3 × **6** = 18
18 is more than 17.
Choose 5 as the quotient.

17 ones ÷ 3 = 5 ones with 2 ones left over

= ⬚ R ⬚

Quotient = ⬚ ones

Remainder = ⬚ ones

17 ÷ 3 = ⬚ R ⬚

Each friend has ⬚ starfish.

b How many starfish are left over?

⬚ starfish are left over.

Find the Remainder!

Players: 2 to 4
Materials:
- pasta pieces
- number cards from 10 to 35
- spinner with numbers 3, 4, and 5

STEP 1 Mix up the number cards. Player 1 turns over a card.

STEP 2 Player 1 takes the number of pasta pieces shown on the card. For example, for the number card 32, take 32 pasta pieces.

STEP 3 Spin the spinner.

STEP 4 Divide the pasta pieces by the number shown on the spinner, and find the remainder.
For example, if Player 1 spins a 5:
- he rearranges the 32 pasta pieces into 5 equal groups, and
- counts the pieces in each group, and the remaining pieces.

The quotient is 6.
The remainder is 2.

STEP 5 Your score is the remainder you get. The other players check the answer using division.

STEP 6 Players take turns to play two rounds each.

> The player with the most points wins!

Guided Learning

Find the missing numbers.

2 20 ones ÷ 3 = [ ] R [ ]

Quotient = [ ] ones

Remainder = [ ] ones

3 43 ones ÷ 5 = [ ] R [ ]

Quotient = [ ] ones

Remainder = [ ] ones

Let's Practice

Find the missing numbers.

1 16 ones ÷ 4 = [ ]

Quotient = [ ] ones

Remainder = [ ] ones

2 15 ones ÷ 2 = [ ] R [ ]

Quotient = [ ] ones

Remainder = [ ] one

3 41 ÷ 5 = [ ] R [ ]

4 33 ÷ 4 = [ ] R [ ]

5 29 ÷ 3 = [ ] R [ ]

Think of the multiplication facts for 2.

6 × 2 = [ ]

7 × 2 = [ ]

8 × 2 = [ ]

Choose [ ] as the quotient.

ON YOUR OWN

Go to Workbook A:
Practice 2, pages 149–150

Lesson 8.3 Odd and Even Numbers

Lesson Objective

- Use different strategies to identify odd and even numbers.

Vocabulary
even numbers
odd numbers

Learn **Use building blocks to identify odd and even numbers.**

Use building blocks to make this pattern.

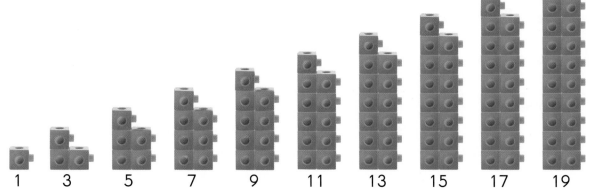

| 1 | 3 | 5 | 7 | 9 | 11 | 13 | 15 | 17 | 19 |

These numbers are odd numbers.

> **Odd numbers** have 1, 3, 5, 7, or 9 in the ones place.

Use building blocks to make this pattern.

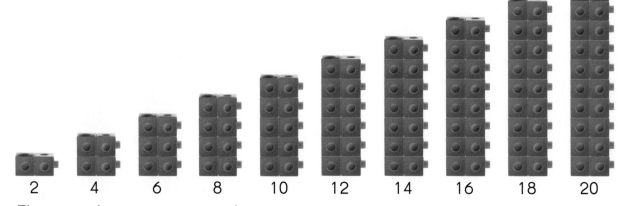

| 2 | 4 | 6 | 8 | 10 | 12 | 14 | 16 | 18 | 20 |

These numbers are even numbers.

> **Even numbers** have 2, 4, 6, 8, or 0 in the ones place.

Divide by 2 to identify odd and even numbers.

Look at this group of odd numbers.

ODD
13 17 19

Divide each number by 2.

Example

13 ÷ 2 = 6 R 1
17 ÷ 2 = 8 R 1
19 ÷ 2 = 9 R 1

What do you notice?

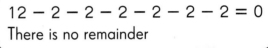
13 − 2 − 2 − 2 − 2 − 2 − 2 = 1
There is a remainder.

When an odd number is divided by 2,
there is always a remainder of 1.

Look at this group of even numbers.

EVEN
12 16 20

Divide each number by 2.

Example

12 ÷ 2 = 6
16 ÷ 2 = 8
20 ÷ 2 = 10

What do you notice?

12 − 2 − 2 − 2 − 2 − 2 − 2 = 0
There is no remainder

When an even number is divided by
2, there is no remainder.

When 0 is divided by 2, there is no remainder.
0 is also an even number.

Guided Learning

Solve.

1. Look at the numbers below. Decide whether each number is odd or even without dividing.

   8   17   26   38   77   129

   Explain your answers. ⬜

Let's Practice

Solve.

1. Is 23 an even number? Explain your answer. ⬜

Divide each number by 2.
Then decide if the number is odd or even.

2. 21 ÷ 2 = ⬜

   21 is a/an ⬜ number.

3. 18 ÷ 2 = ⬜

   18 is a/an ⬜ number.

ON YOUR OWN

Go to Workbook A:
Practice 3, pages 151–152

Division Without Remainder and Regrouping

Lesson Objective

- Use base-ten blocks and place value to divide 2-digit numbers without regrouping or remainders.

Learn **Use partial products to divide.**

3 friends share 63 squashes equally.
How many squashes does each friend get?
$63 \div 3 = ?$

Tens	Ones

Step 1

Divide the **tens** by 3.

6 tens $\div$ 3 = 2 tens

```
  T O
  2
3)6 3
  6 0  ← 3 × 2 tens
```

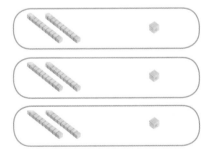

Step 2

Divide the **ones** by 3.

3 ones $\div$ 3 = 1 one

So, $63 \div 3 = 21$.

```
   2 1  ← Quotient
 3)6 3
   6 0
     3
     3  ← 3 × 1 one
     0  ← Remainder
```

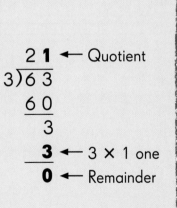

Each friend gets 21 squashes.

Guided Learning

Solve.

1 3 friends share 39 tomatoes equally.
How many tomatoes does each friend get?

$39 \div 3 = ?$

Tens	Ones

Step 1
Divide the **tens** by 3.

3 tens $\div$ 3 = [ ] ten

```
    T O
     1
3) 3 9
   3 0
```

Tens	Ones

Step 2
Divide the **ones** by 3.

9 ones $\div$ 3 = [ ] ones

So, 39 $\div$ 3 = [ ].

Each friend gets

[ ] tomatoes.

```
    1 3
3) 3 9
   3 0
     9
     9
     0
```

Divide. Use base-ten blocks to help you.

2 48 ÷ 2 = ?

Step 1 Divide the tens.

[   ] tens ÷ 2 = [   ] tens

Step 2 Divide the ones.

[   ] ones ÷ [   ] = [   ] ones

So, 48 ÷ 2 = [   ].

3 Find 69 ÷ 3 = ?

Step 1 Divide the tens.

[   ] tens ÷ [   ] = [   ] tens

Step 2 Divide the ones.

[   ] ones ÷ [   ] = [   ] ones

So, 69 ÷ 3 = [   ].

Divide. Use base-ten blocks to help you.

4 4)4 8

5 5)5 5

6 2)6 4

7 3)9 0

8 4)8 4

9 3)6 6

Let's Practice

Divide. Use base-ten blocks to help you.

1 9 ones ÷ 3 = [ ] ones

2 5 tens ÷ 5 = [ ] tens

3 8 tens ÷ 4 = [ ] tens

4 6 ones ÷ 2 = [ ] ones

Divide. Use base-ten blocks to help you.

5 96 ÷ 3 = ?

Divide the tens.

9 tens ÷ 3 = [ ] tens

Divide the ones.

6 ones ÷ 3 = [ ] ones

So, 96 ÷ 3 = [ ].

Divide. Use base-ten blocks to help you.

6
[ ] [ ]
3)9 6

7
[ ] [ ]
2)8 2

8
[ ] [ ]
4)4 8

9
[ ] [ ]
5)5 0

Solve.

10 Rebecca buys 44 tennis balls.
She packs the tennis balls equally into 4 bags.
How many tennis balls does Rebecca pack into each bag? [ ]

11 Fernando has 84 marbles.
He divides the marbles equally into 2 groups.
How many marbles are there in each group?
[ ]

ON YOUR OWN

**Go to Workbook A:
Practice 4, pages 153–154**

Division with Regrouping in Tens and Ones

Lesson 8.5

Lesson Objective

- Use base-ten blocks and place value to divide a 2-digit number by a 1-digit number with regrouping, with or without remainders.

Learn **Regroup to divide.**

Jason and Brad collect rocks. They share 32 rocks equally.
How many rocks does each boy get?

$32 \div 2 = ?$

Tens	Ones

Step 1

Divide the **tens** by 2.

3 tens ÷ 2
= 1 ten with
1 ten left over

```
    T O
    1
 2)3 2
    2 0  ← 2 × 1 ten
    1
```

Tens	Ones

Regroup the
1 ten left over.
1 ten = 10 ones

Add the ones.
10 ones + 2 ones
= 12 ones

```
    1
 2)3 2
    2 0
    1 2
```

Tens	Ones

Step 2

Divide the **ones** by 2.
12 ones ÷ 2
= 6 ones

```
    1 6
 2)3 2
    2 0
    1 2
    1 2  ← 2 × 6 ones
      0
```

So, $32 \div 2 = 16$.
Each boy gets 16 rocks.

Guided Learning

Solve.

1 3 friends share 56 trading cards equally.
How many cards does each boy get?
How many cards are left over?

$56 \div 3 = ?$

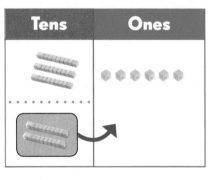

Tens	Ones

Step 1

Divide the **tens** by 3.
5 tens ÷ 3

= [ ] ten with

remainder [ ] tens

Tens	Ones

Regroup the remainder tens.
2 tens = 20 ones
Add the ones.
20 ones + 6 ones
= 26 ones

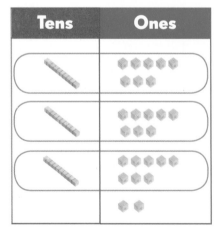

Tens	Ones

Step 2

Divide the **ones** by 3.

[ ] ones ÷ 3

= [ ] ones with

remainder [ ] ones

So, $56 \div 3$
= [ ] R [ ].

Each friend gets [ ] cards.

[ ] cards are left over.

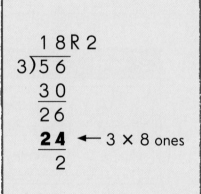

T O

1
3)5 6
3 0   ← 3 × 1 ten
2

1
3)5 6
3 0
2 6

1 8 R 2
3)5 6
3 0
2 6
2 4   ← 3 × 8 ones
2

Hands-On Activity

WORK IN PAIRS

Use base-ten blocks to help you divide!

Regroup each remainder ten into 10 ones.

a Divide 7 tens 2 ones between 2 children.

b Divide 5 tens and 7 ones into 3 baskets.

c Divide 9 tens and 6 ones among 4 families.

Guided Learning

Divide. Use base-ten blocks to help you.

2 4)5 6

3 5)7 5

4 2)7 9

Solve. Use base-ten blocks to help you.

5 Mr. Ross divides 63 books into stacks of 5.

a How many stacks are there? ☐

b How many books are left over? ☐

Let's Practice

Divide.

1 18 ones ÷ 2 = ◻ ones

2 18 ones ÷ 3 = ◻ ones

3 15 ones ÷ 3 = ◻ ones

4 15 ones ÷ 5 = ◻ ones

Find the missing numbers.

5 96 = 8 tens ◻ ones

6 54 = ◻ tens 24 ones

Divide. Give the remainder in tens. Use base-ten blocks to help you.

7 5 tens ÷ 2 = ◻ tens with remainder ◻ ten

8 8 tens ÷ 3 = ◻ tens with remainder ◻ tens

Divide. Give the remainder in ones. Use base-ten blocks to help you.

9 5 tens ÷ 3 = ◻ ten with remainder ◻ ones

10 7 tens ÷ 4 = ◻ ten with remainder ◻ ones

Divide.

11

$$2\overline{)3\ 4}$$

12

$$3\overline{)5\ 1}$$

Solve.

13 Timothy packs 60 bottles of orange juice equally into 4 coolers.
How many bottles are in each cooler? ◻

ON YOUR OWN

**Go to Workbook A:
Practice 5, page 155**

Put On Your Thinking Cap!

PROBLEM SOLVING

Find the missing numbers.

1

```
      4 5
  2) 9 ▢
      8 0
      1 0
      1 0
        0
```

2

```
     ▢ ▢
  5) 7 ▢
     5 0
     2 6
     2 5
       1
```

3

```
       1 7
  ▢) 6 ▢
     4 0
     2 ▢
     ▢ ▢
       1
```

4

```
     ▢ ▢
  ▢) 9 ▢
     6 0
     3 0
       ▢
       0
```

ON YOUR OWN

**Go to Workbook A:
Put On Your Thinking Cap!
pages 157–158**

Chapter Wrap Up

Study Guide

You have learned...

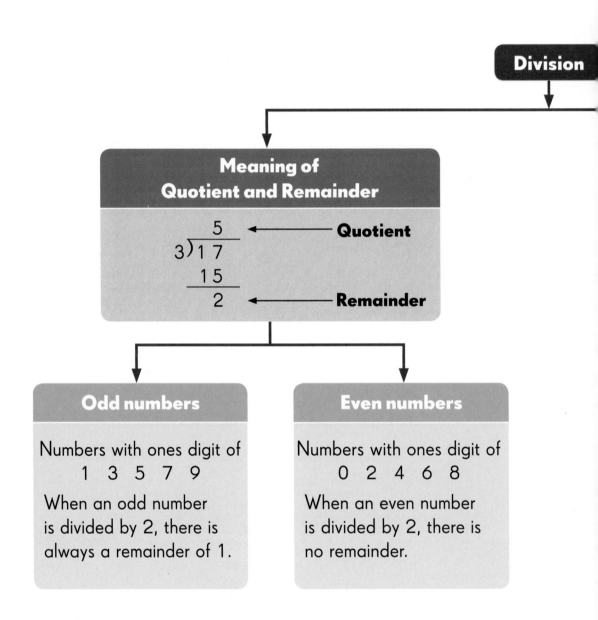

Division

Meaning of Quotient and Remainder

$$\begin{array}{r} 5 \\ 3{\overline{\smash{\big)}\,1\,7}} \\ \underline{1\,5} \\ 2 \end{array}$$

5 ← Quotient

2 ← Remainder

Odd numbers

Numbers with ones digit of
1 3 5 7 9

When an odd number is divided by 2, there is always a remainder of 1.

Even numbers

Numbers with ones digit of
0 2 4 6 8

When an even number is divided by 2, there is no remainder.

▶ There can be remainders when dividing to make equal groups or when sharing equally.

Divide		
Mentally by recalling multiplication facts	**A 2-digit number by a 1-digit number (without regrouping)**	**A 2-digit number by a 1-digit number (with regrouping)**
Find $90 \div 3$. $90 \div 3 = 9$ tens $\div 3$ $ = 3$ tens $ = 30$ So, $90 \div 3 = 30$. Find $900 \div 3$. $900 \div 3 = 9$ hundreds $\div 3$ $ = 3$ hundreds $ = 300$ So, $900 \div 3 = 300$.	$$\begin{array}{r} 1\,2 \\ 4\overline{)4\,8} \\ \underline{4\,0} \leftarrow 4 \times 1 \text{ ten} \\ 8 \\ \underline{8} \leftarrow 4 \times 2 \text{ ones} \\ 0 \end{array}$$	$$\begin{array}{r} 2\,5 \\ 3\overline{)7\,5} \\ \underline{6\,0} \leftarrow 3 \times 2 \text{ tens} \\ 1\,5 \\ \underline{1\,5} \leftarrow 3 \times 5 \text{ ones} \\ 0 \end{array}$$

Chapter Review/Test

Vocabulary
Choose the correct word.

> even
> remainder
> odd
> quotient

1 The answer in a division problem is called a ___ .

2 When an ___ number is divided by 2, there is always a ___ of 1.

3 When an ___ number is divided by 2, there is no remainder.

Concepts and Skills
Find the missing numbers.

4 ___ × 5 = 30

30 ÷ 5 = ___

5 ___ × 3 = 21

21 ÷ 3 = ___

6 ___ × 4 = 36

36 ÷ 4 = ___

Divide. Use related multiplication facts to help you.

7 54 ÷ 6 = ___   6 × ___ = 54

540 ÷ 6 = ___

5,400 ÷ 6 = ___

8 35 ÷ 7 = ___   7 × ___ = 35

350 ÷ 7 = ___

3,500 ÷ 7 = ___

Divide.

9 44 ÷ 4 = [ ]

10 86 ÷ 2 = [ ]

11 93 ÷ 3 = [ ]

12 38 ÷ 2 = [ ]

13 54 ÷ 3 = [ ]

14 72 ÷ 4 = [ ]

15 65 ÷ 5 = [ ]

16 43 ÷ 3 = [ ]

17 59 ÷ 4 = [ ]

18 99 ÷ 5 = [ ]

Problem Solving

19 A farmer has 36 sheep. He has 4 sheep pens.
He keeps an equal number of sheep in each pen.
How many sheep does each pen have? [ ]

20 Lisa bakes 45 muffins.
She puts the muffins equally into 3 boxes.
How many muffins are in each box? [ ]

21 Sharon needs 69 plastic butterflies for her mobiles.
She puts 4 plastic butterflies on each mobile.

a How many mobiles does she have? [ ]

b How many butterflies are left over? [ ]

22 Paul has 58 bicycles in his shop.
He arranges them in 5 equal rows.

a How many bicycles are in each row? [ ]

b How many bicycles are left over? [ ]

9 Using Bar Models: Multiplication and Division

How many children are on the red mats? How many children are on the yellow mat?

Lessons

9.1 Real-World Problems: Multiplication

9.2 Real-World Problems: Two-Step Problems with Multiplication

9.3 Real-World Problems: Division

9.4 Real-World Problems: Two-Step Problems with Division

BIG IDEA

▶ Bar models can be used to solve different kinds of multiplication and division word problems.

Recall Prior Knowledge

Using bar models to solve multiplication problems

Multiply 4 by 3.

4 × 3 = 12

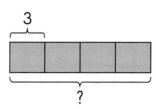

Using bar models to solve division problems

① Divide 24 by 3.

24 ÷ 3 = 8

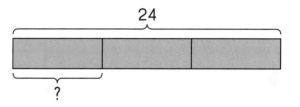

② Divide 14 into groups of 2.

14 ÷ 2 = 7

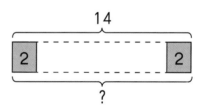

✔ Quick Check

Complete each multiplication sentence. Use bar models to help you.

①

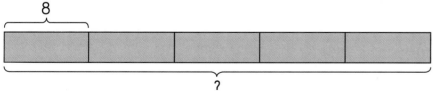

[ ] × [ ] = [ ]

Complete each multiplication sentence. Use the bar model to help you.

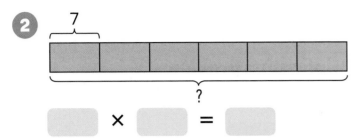

2

$$\boxed{} \times \boxed{} = \boxed{}$$

Complete each division sentence. Use the bar model to help you.

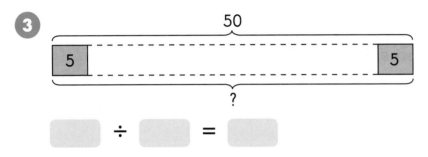

3

$$\boxed{} \div \boxed{} = \boxed{}$$

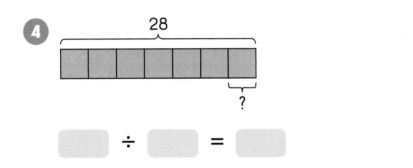

4

$$\boxed{} \div \boxed{} = \boxed{}$$

Draw bar models.

5 $4 \times 9 = ?$

6 $56 \div 8 = ?$

Real-World Problems: Multiplication

Lesson Objective

- Use bar models to solve one-step multiplication word problems.

Vocabulary
twice

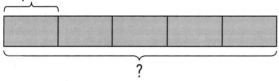 **Use bar models to solve one-step multiplication word problems.**

There are 5 boxes of pencils.
Each box contains 12 pencils.
How many pencils are there in all?

12 pencils

?

1 unit ⟶ 12

5 units ⟶ 5 × 12 = 60

There are 60 pencils in all.

Guided Learning

Solve. Use bar models to help you.

1 Mark pays $195 a month for rent.
How much rent does he pay in all for 3 months?

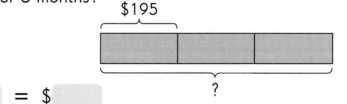

$195

?

1 unit ⟶ $ [ ]

3 units ⟶ $ [ ] × [ ] = $ [ ]

He pays $ [ ] in all for 3 months.

Learn Use bar models to solve one-step multiplication word problems.

Zach has 342 stamps.
Ron has **twice** as many stamps as Zach.
How many stamps does Ron have?

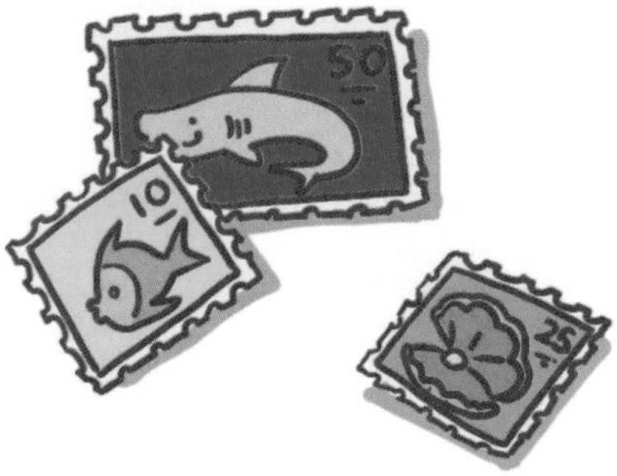

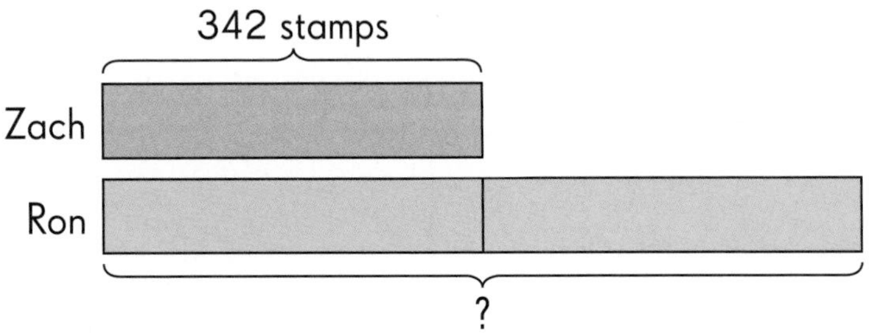

342 × 2 = 684

Ron has 684 stamps.

Twice is 2 times.

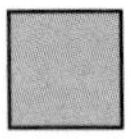 stands for 342 stamps.

So, 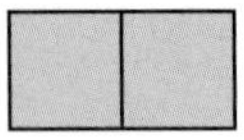 stands for 342 stamps × 2.

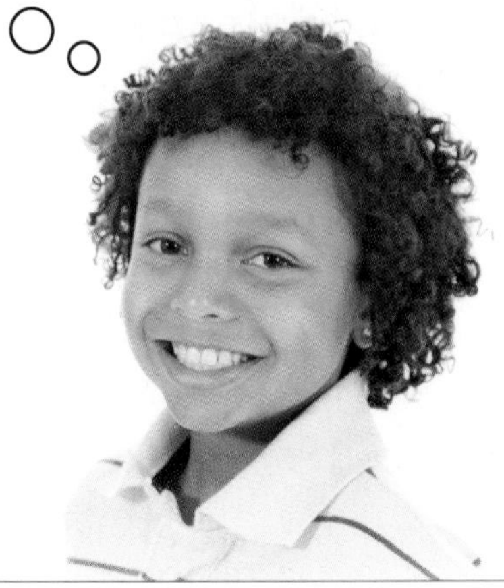

Guided Learning

Solve. Use the bar models to help you.

2 The Garden Center sells 250 packs of seeds.
Fran's Nursery sells 3 times as many packs of seeds as the Garden Center.
How many packs of seeds does Fran's Nursery sell?

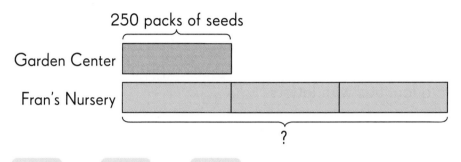

☐ × ☐ = ☐

Fran's Nursery sells ☐ packs of seeds.

☐ stands for 250 packs of seeds

So, ☐☐☐ stands for 250 packs of seeds × 3.

Let's Practice

Solve. Draw bar models to help you.

1 On Monday, Mrs. Bollat sells 424 movie tickets.
On Tuesday, she sells twice as many tickets as on Monday.
How many tickets does she sell on Tuesday? ☐

2 A newsstand has 7 boxes of magazines.
Each box contains 120 magazines.
How many magazines does the newsstand have in all? ☐

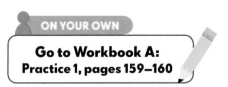

ON YOUR OWN

Go to Workbook A:
Practice 1, pages 159–160

Real-World Problems: Two-Step Problems with Multiplication

Lesson Objectives

- Use bar models to solve two-step word problems.
- Choose the correct operations to solve two-step word problems.
- Represent unknown quantities with letters.

ᴸᵉᵃʳⁿ **Use bar models to solve two-step word problems.**

Gas Station A sells 273 gallons of gas in the morning. On the same morning, Gas Station B sells double the amount of gas that Gas Station A sells.

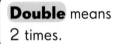
Double means 2 times.

a How many gallons of gas does Gas Station B sell?

b How many gallons of gas do they sell in all?

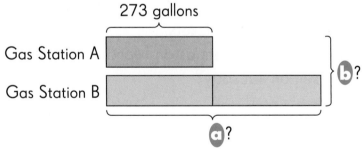

a 273 × 2 = 546
Gas Station B sells 546 gallons of gas.

b 273 + 546 = 819
They sell 819 gallons of gas in all.

Guided Learning

Solve. Use the bar models to help you.

1 A bookstore had 4 shelves of books.
Each shelf had 116 books.
The store owner sold 382 books.
How many books were left?

First, find the total number of books.

116 books

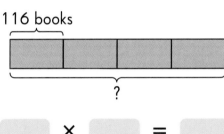

?

[ ] × [ ] = [ ]

There were [ ] books at first.

[ ] books

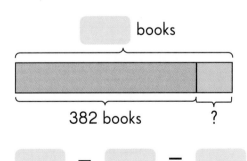

382 books   ?

[ ] – [ ] = [ ]

There were [ ] books left.

Solve. Use the bar models to help you.

2 Randy has some oranges and apples.
He puts 2 oranges and 3 apples into each box.
He has a total of 6 boxes of fruit.
How many pieces of fruit does Randy have in all?

[ ] + [ ] = [ ]

There are [ ] pieces of fruit in each box.

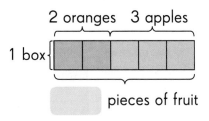

2 oranges   3 apples

1 box [ ][ ][ ][ ][ ]

[ ] pieces of fruit

[ ] pieces of fruit

[ ][ ][ ][ ][ ][ ]
?

1 unit ⟶ [ ]

6 units ⟶ [ ] × 5 = [ ]

Randy has [ ] pieces of fruit in all.

3 Flo saves 4 times as much money as Larry.
Maria saves $12 less than Flo.
Larry saves $32.
How much money does Maria save?

1 unit ⟶ $[ ]

4 units ⟶ $[ ] × [ ] = $[ ]

Flo saves $[ ].

$[ ] − $[ ] = $[ ]

Maria saves $[ ].

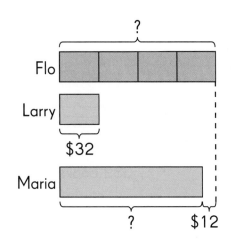

?

Flo [ ][ ][ ][ ]

Larry [ ]

$32

Maria [ ]

? $12

Learn Use letters to represent unknown numbers.

When you draw a bar model, you can use a variable in place of a question mark. When you need to find two numbers in a problem, you can use a different variable for each number.

1 Jack has 4 boxes of mangoes for sale.
Each box contains 12 mangoes.
Kathy bought 25 mangoes from Jack.

a How many mangoes does Jack have for sale?

$4 \times 12 = ?$
$4 \times 12 = x$

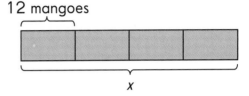
12 mangoes

The letter x represents the number of mangoes Jack has for sale.

$x = 48$

Jack has 48 mangoes for sale.

b How many mangoes does Jack have left?

$48 - 25 = ?$
$48 - 25 = y$

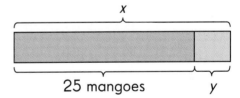
25 mangoes   y

The letter y represents the number of mangoes Jake has left.

$y = 23$

Jack has 23 mangoes left.

You use two different letters in this problem because there are two numbers you do not know.

Guided Learning

Use the letters *d* and *e* to represent the unknown numbers. Complete and solve.

4 Miguel buys 4 boxes of carrots.
Each box contains 24 carrots.
The carrots are used to bake 8 carrot cakes.
How many carrots are used in each cake?

24 carrots

[ ] × [ ] = [ ]

d = [ ]

Miguel buys [ ] carrots.

[ ] ÷ [ ] = [ ]

e = [ ]

There are [ ] carrots used in each cake.

Let's Practice

Decide whether to add, subtract, multiply, or divide at each step. Then solve the word problem. Draw bar models to help you.

1 One bag of peanuts costs $5.
Alicia wants to buy 8 bags of peanuts
but she has only $33.
How much more money does she need? [ ]

2 Megan makes a necklace with 12 red beads
and 15 yellow beads.
She makes a total of 3 necklaces.
How many beads does she use in all?

Solve each problem using bar models and variables.

3 Sandy has $60.
She wants to buy 7 teddy bears.
If each teddy bear cost $6, how much
money does she have left?

4 Pat is 12 years old.
James is 3 times as old as Pat.
Raymond is 9 years younger than James.
How old is Raymond?

5 Michael buys 4 packets of ham.
Each packet costs $6.
He has $18 with him.
How much more money does he need?

6 Gemma, Ricky, and Kim each spends $16 at the bookstore.
Elesha spends $12 less than their total.
How much money does Elesha spend?

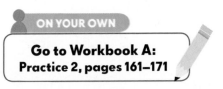

ON YOUR OWN

**Go to Workbook A:
Practice 2, pages 161–171**

Math Journal

WORKING TOGETHER

Write a two-step word problem using these words and numbers. Then draw bar models and solve it.

1

| twice as many | breadsticks | 745 |

| How many | in all | Jennifer | Manuel |

These are bar models drawn for another word problem. Write a two-step word problem for the bar models.

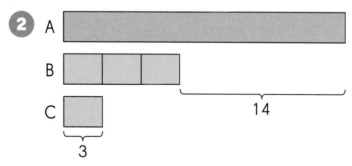

2 A

B

C

3

14

Lesson 9.3 Real-World Problems: Division

Lesson Objectives

- Use bar models to solve one-step division word problems.
- Recognize number relationships.

Learn Use bar models to solve one-step division word problems.

A grower picks 60 oranges.
The grower packs them equally into 5 boxes.
How many oranges does the grower pack in each box?

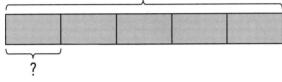
60 oranges
?

$$60 \div 5 = 12$$

He packs 12 oranges in each box.

Guided Learning

Solve. Use bar models to help you.

1 There are 48 crayons.
They are packed equally into 4 boxes.
How many crayons does each box have?

☐ ÷ ☐ = ☐

Each box has ☐ crayons.

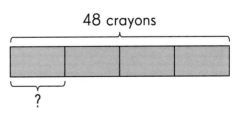
48 crayons
?

Solve. Use bar models to help you.

2 A tricycle has 3 wheels.
There are 42 tricycle wheels in Jerome's shop.
How many tricycles does Jerome have?

42 ÷ [　　] = [　　]

There are [　　] tricycles in Jerome's shop.

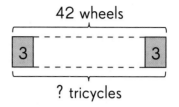
42 wheels

3 [- - - - - - -] 3

? tricycles

Use bar models to solve one-step division word problems.

Shawn and Trish scored 36 goals in all.
Shawn scored 3 times as many goals as Trish.
How many goals did Trish score?

4 units ⟶ 36
1 unit ⟶ 36 ÷ 4 = 9

Trish scored 9 goals.

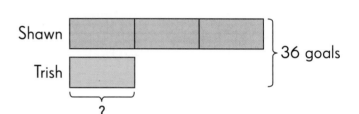

Shawn

Trish

} 36 goals

?

Guided Learning

Solve. Use bar models to help you.

3 Jake sells 32 video games.
He sells 4 times as many video games as Justin.
How many video games does Justin sell?

[　　] units ⟶ [　　]

[　　] unit ⟶ [　　] ÷ [　　]

= [　　]

Justin sells [　　] video games.

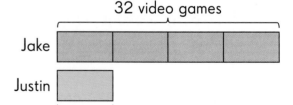

32 video games

Jake

Justin

?

Let's Practice

Solve. Draw bar models to help you.

1 Mr. Lee packs 80 pounds of rice into 5-pound bags.
How many bags does he use?

2 During a school fair, Daniel sells 87 cups of juice.
He sells 3 times as many cups of juice as Rodney.
How many cups of juice does Rodney sell?

3 The total age of Melvin and Jack is 72 years.
Melvin is 3 times as old as Jack.
How old is Jack?

4 Darren uses 4 pieces of wood to make 1 picture frame.
How many frames can he make with 72 pieces of wood?

5 A bowling alley has 81 bowling balls.
Each lane has 9 balls beside it.
How many lanes does the bowling alley have?

ON YOUR OWN

Go to Workbook A:
Practice 3, pages 173–176

9.4 Real-World Problems: Two-Step Problems with Division

Lesson Objectives

- Use bar models to solve two-step word problems.
- Choose the correct operations to solve two-step word problems.
- Solve two-step word problems using the four operations.
- Represent unknown quantities with letters.

Learn Use bar models to solve two-step word problems.

A baker has 28 ounces of flour.
He uses 8 ounces of it to make biscuits.
He packs the remaining flour equally into 5 bags.

a How much flour is left?

b How many ounces of flour does each bag have?

a $28 - 8 = 20$

20 ounces of flour is left.

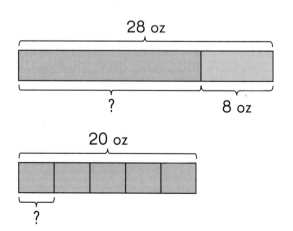

b $20 \div 5 = 4$

Each bag has 4 ounces of flour.

Guided Learning

Solve. Use bar models to help you.

1 Joel buys 3 boxes of pencils. Each box contains 32 pencils.
The pencils are shared equally among 4 children.
How many pencils does each child get?

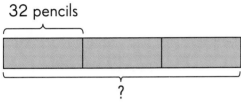

32 pencils

?

First, find out how many
pencils Joel buys.

32 × 3 = ⬜

Joel buys ⬜ pencils.

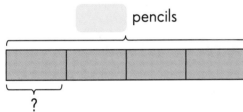

⬜ pencils

?

Then find out how many
pencils each child gets.

96 ÷ 4 = ⬜

Each child gets ⬜ pencils.

2 Rodrigo buys 3 boxes of buttons. Each box contains 16 buttons.
He packs the buttons into bags of 8 buttons each.
How many bags of buttons does he have?

⬜ × ⬜ = ⬜

Rodrigo has ⬜ buttons.

⬜ ÷ ⬜ = ⬜

He has ⬜ bags of buttons.

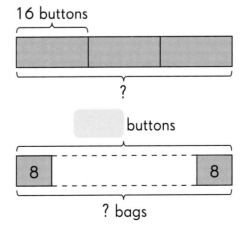

16 buttons

?

⬜ buttons

8   8

? bags

3 Jackie, Kim, and Minah have 55 stamps in all.
Jackie has twice as many stamps as Kim.
Minah has 10 stamps.
How many stamps does Kim have?

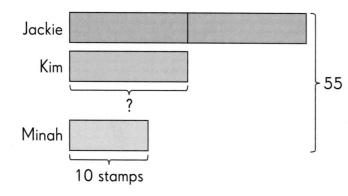

Jackie
Kim
?
Minah
10 stamps
55 stamps

[   ] − [   ] = [   ]

Jackie and Kim have [   ] stamps.

3 units ⟶ [   ]

1 unit ⟶ [   ] ÷ 3 = [   ]

Kim has [   ] stamps.

Use a letter instead of a ? to represent an unknown number.

Fiona has 30 ounces of rice.
She uses 10 ounces to make a rice salad.
She packs the remaining rice into bags.
Each bag has 5 ounces of rice.

a How much rice does she have left?

$$30 - 10 = ?$$
$$30 - 10 = b$$

The letter b represents the amount of rice Fiona has left.

$$b = 20 \text{ ounces}$$

Fiona has 20 ounces of rice left.

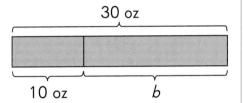

b How many bags of rice does she pack?

$$20 \div 5 = c$$

The letter c represents the number of bags of rice.

$$c = 4$$

Fiona packs 4 bags of rice.

You use two different letters in this problem because there are two numbers you do not know.

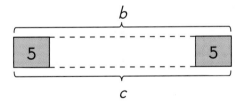

Guided Learning

Solve. Use letters to represent the unknown numbers.

4 Nina has 128 stamps.
She gives 36 to Sam and divides the rest among 4 people.

a How many stamps does Nina have left?

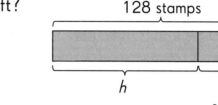

128 stamps

h   36
        stamps

[ ] − [ ] = [ ]

[ ] − [ ] = [ ]

The letter [ ] represents the number of stamps left.

h = [ ]

Nina has [ ] stamps left.

b How many stamps does each person have?

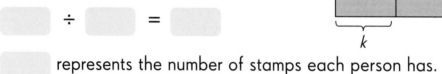

92 stamps

k

[ ] ÷ [ ] = [ ]

[ ] represents the number of stamps each person has.

k = [ ]

Each person has [ ] stamps.

Let's Practice

Decide whether to add, subtract, multiply, or divide at each step. Then solve the word problem. Draw bar models to help you.

1 Joe has 32 envelopes and Pete has 48 envelopes.
They share the envelopes equally.

a How many envelopes do they have in all?

b How many envelopes does each of them have?

2 Naomi has 29 biscuits.
She gives Charlie 9 biscuits.
She divides the rest of the biscuits among 5 people.
How many biscuits does each person have?

3 Dina, Sue, and Kelley have $98 in all.
Dina has 4 times as much money as Kelley.
Sue has $18.
How much money does Kelley have?

4 Adam, Ben, Carlos, and Darren share a $96 bill for dinner equally.
They each also tip the waitress $2.
How much does each of them spend in all?

Solve. Use letters to represent the unknown numbers.

5 James, Mark, and Lisa share $84 for a charity ticket.
Mark has $48 left.
How much does Mark have at the beginning?

6 Bill has 74 marbles. His father buys him another 74. He shares these marbles among his 4 friends. How many marbles does each of them have?

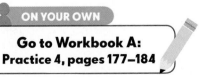

ON YOUR OWN

Go to Workbook A:
Practice 4, pages 177–184

WORKING TOGETHER

Write two-step word problems using these words and numbers. Then solve. Use bar models to help you.

1

| Vincent | breadsticks | shared equally | Tony |

| altogether | 45 | How many | 21 |

These are bar models drawn for another word problem. Write a two-step word problem for the bar models. Then solve it.

2

A
B
C

Put On Your Thinking Cap!

PROBLEM SOLVING

Solve. Use the bar models to help you.

1 Mr. King has a total of 19 geese, chickens, and ducks on his farm.
He has 3 more chickens than geese.
He has 2 fewer ducks than geese.
How many ducks does he have?

Use the **bar model** to help you solve the problem.

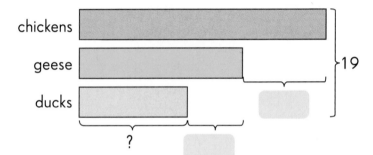

2 Gita puts tires on 21 bicycles and tricycles.
She uses 53 tires in all.
How many tricycles are there?

ON YOUR OWN

**Go to Workbook A:
Put On Your Thinking Cap!
pages 187–188**

Chapter Wrap Up

Study Guide
You have learned...

> **Using Bar Models : Multiplication and Division**

> **One-Step**

Multiplication

Chloe has 3 boxes of hair clips.
Each box has 12 hair clips.
How many hair clips does Chloe have in all?

12 hair clips

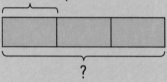

$12 \times 3 = 36$
Chloe has 36 hair clips in all.

Division

Tom has 42 toy soldiers.
He keeps them equally in 3 drawers.
How many toy soldiers are there in each drawer?

42 toy soldiers

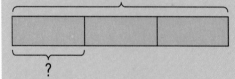

?

3 units ⟶ 42
1 unit ⟶ $42 \div 3 = 14$
There are 14 toy soldiers in each drawer.

Clark divides 72 stamps equally among the pages of his album.
Each page has 8 stamps.
How many pages of the album has stamps?

72 stamps

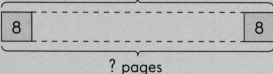

? pages

$72 \div 8 = 9$
9 pages of the album has stamps.

▶ Bar models can be used to solve
different kinds of multiplication and
division word problems.

Two-Step

Multiplication

Josie has 4 black T-shirts.
She has 3 times as many white as
black T-shirts. How many T-shirts
does she have in all?

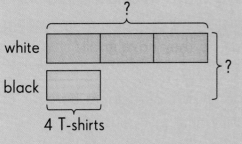

$3 \times 4 = 12$

$12 + 4 = 16$

Josie has 16 T-shirts in all.

Division

Elsie divides 20 paper clips equally
among 4 girls. She then gives each girl 2
more paper clips. How many paper clips
does each girl have?

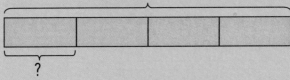

$20 \div 4 = 5$

$5 + 2 = 7$

Each girl has 7 paper clips.

Multiplication and Division

Douglas has 4 boxes of pencils.
Each box has 10 pencils.
He gives the pencils to 8 children.
How many pencils does each child get?

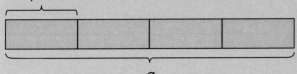

$4 \times 10 = a$

$a = 40$

He has 40 pencils.

$40 \div 8 = b$

$b = 5$

Each child gets 5 pencils.

Chapter Review/Test

Vocabulary

Choose the correct word.

1. When we ☐ 5 by 2, we get a product of 10.

2. Two times a number is ☐ or ☐ that number.

divide
twice
multiply
double

Concepts and Skills

Match each model to a word problem. Then solve the problem.

3. 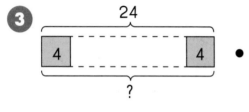 •

   • Lynn has 4 times as many trading cards as Linda. Linda has 4 trading cards. How many trading cards do they have in all? **A**

4. 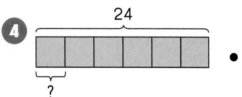 •

   • Linda shares 24 trading cards equally among 4 girls. How many trading cards does each girl receive? **B**

5. 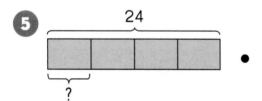 •

   • Linda has 6 packs of trading cards. There are 8 trading cards in each pack. How many trading cards are there in all? **C**

6. 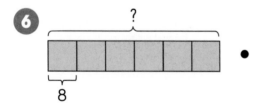 •

   • Linda has 24 trading cards. She packs them into 6 packs equally. How many trading cards does each pack have? **D**

7. 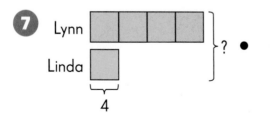 •

   • Lynn has 24 trading cards. She gives 4 trading cards each to some girls. How many girls are there? **E**

Problem Solving

Solve.

8 Andrea has 6 vases.
She puts 3 roses and 4 lilies in each vase.
How many flowers are there in all?

9 A carpenter orders 84 doors.
He orders 3 times as many red doors as blue doors.
How many blue doors does he order?

Solve. Use letters to represent the unknown numbers.

10 Tim has 8 pieces of wood.
He saws each piece into 5 smaller pieces.
He then packs them equally into 4 bundles.
How many pieces of wood does each bundle have?

11 There are 51 children at a party.
A clown brings some balloons to the party.
He bursts 15 balloons while trying to inflate them.
How many balloons does he bring if each child receives 3 balloons?

Glossary

- **area model of multiplication**

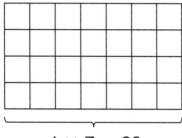

$$4 \times 7 = 28$$

- **array model of multiplication**

An array model of multiplication is an arrangement in rows and columns.

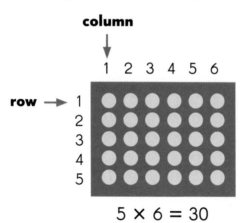

$$5 \times 6 = 30$$

- **Associative Property of Multiplication**

Changing the way numbers in a multiplication sentence are grouped and multiplied does not change the answer.

$$\mathbf{3} \times \mathbf{2} \times 5 = \mathbf{6} \times 5$$
$$= 30$$
$$3 \times \mathbf{2} \times \mathbf{5} = 3 \times \mathbf{10}$$
$$= 30$$

B

- **bar model**

  The bar model helps to solve word problems.
  Bars are drawn, labelled with all the relevant information, and divided according to the situation in the word problem.

  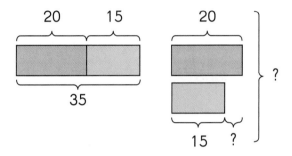

C

- **Commutative Property of Multiplication**

  Changing the order of numbers in a multiplication sentence does not change the answer.
  10 × 2 = 20
  2 × 10 = 20

  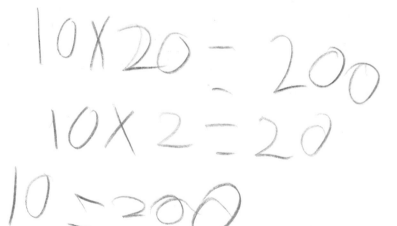

D

- **difference**

  The difference is the answer to a subtraction problem.
  $1,047 - 23 = 1,024$,
  1,024 is the difference between 1,047 and 23.

- **digit**

  A number is made up of digits.
  In the number 1,479, the digits are 1, 4, 7, and 9.

- **division**

  Division is an operation of making equal groups. It is used to find the number of groups, or the number in each group.

- **dot paper**

  A dot paper shows a set of dots in equal rows and equal columns. It is an example of an array.

  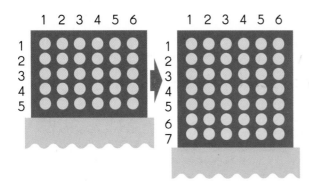

- **double**

  two times

E

- **equal groups**

  These are equal groups.
  They both have the same number of items.

- **estimate**

  An estimate is a number close to the exact number.
  396 is 400 when rounded to the nearest hundred.
  400 is an estimate.

- **even number**

  Any number that has the digit 0, 2, 4, 6, or 8 in its ones place is
  an even number. 12,354 and 7,956 are even numbers.

- **expanded form**

  The expanded form of a number shows the value of each digit in it.
  2,000 + 400 + 70 + 5 is the expanded form of 2,475.

F

- **front-end estimation**

  Front-end estimation uses leading digits to estimate sums and differences.

G ———————

- **greater than (>)**

   Use *greater than* when comparing two numbers.

   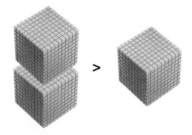

   2,000 > 1,000
   2,000 is greater than 1,000.

- **greatest**

   Use *greatest* when comparing more than two numbers.

   | 2 | 200 | 2,000 |

   2,000 is the greatest number.

L ———————

- **leading digit**

   The leading digit in a number is the digit with the greatest place value.
   The leading digit for **2**,475 is **2**.

- **least**

   Use *least* when comparing more than two numbers.

   | 2 | 200 | 2,000 |

   2 is the least number.

- **less than (<)**

  Use *less than* when comparing two numbers.

  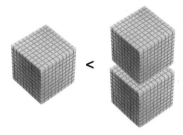

  1,000 < 2,000
  1,000 is less than 2,000.

M——————

- **multiplication**

  Multiplication is an operation of repeated addition. It can be shown by using area, array, and number line models.

- **Multiplicative Property of One**

  Any number multiplied by 1 equals that number.

  2 × 1 = 2   7 × 1 = 7

- **Multiplicative Property of Zero**

  Any number multiplied by 0 equals 0.

  3 × 0 = 0   7 × 0 = 0

N

- **number bond**

  A number bond is a picture that shows the whole of a number and its parts.

  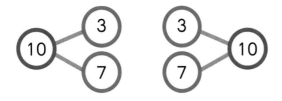

- **number line**

  A number line is a line on which numbers can be located.

  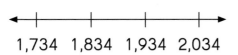

  1,734   1,834   1,934   2,034

O

- **odd number**

  Any number that has the digit 1, 3, 5, 7, or 9 in its ones place is an odd number. 11,203 and 1,245 are odd numbers.

P

- **place value**

  Place value is the value of a digit in a number.
  In 8,769, the digit 8 is in the thousands place.

- **place-value chart**

  A place-value chart is used to show the position and value of a digit in a number.

Thousands	Hundreds	Tens	Ones
8	7	6	9

- **place-value strips**

  Place-value strips show the digits in a number as multiples of 1, 10, 100, and 1,000.

  $$2,000$$
  $$400$$
  $$70$$
  $$5$$

- **product**

  A product is the answer in a multiplication problem.
  $5 \times 7 = 35$
  35 is the product of 5 and 7.

Q

- **quotient**

  A quotient is the answer to a division problem.
  $8 \div 2 = 4$
  4 is the quotient.

R

- **reasonable**

  1,245 + 2,534 = 3,779

  1,245 rounded to the nearest thousand is 1,000.

  2,534 rounded to the nearest thousand is 3,000.

  The estimated sum is 4,000.

  3,779 is close to 4,000 so the answer is reasonable.

- **regroup**

  To regroup means to change:

  10 ones to 1 ten or 1 ten to 10 ones;
  10 tens to 1 hundred or 1 hundred to 10 tens;
  10 hundreds to 1 thousand or 1 thousand to 10 hundreds.

- **remainder**

  A remainder is the number left over from a division problem.

  11 ÷ 2 = 5 R 1
  When 11 is divided by 2, the remainder is 1.

- **repeated addition**

  Repeated addition is adding the same number multiple times.

  (2 × 3) = (2 + 2 + 2)

- **rounded**

  Rounded is the term used in estimating numbers to the nearest ten or hundred.

  2,476 is 2,480 when rounded to the nearest ten.

  2,436 is 2,400 when rounded to the nearest hundred.

  2,456 is 2,500 when rounded to the nearest hundred.

- **rule**

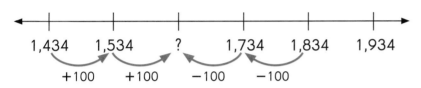

  To find the missing number in the number pattern, the rule is to either add 100 to the number before it or subtract 100 from the number after it.

S

- **share equally**

  To share equally means to separate a set into equal parts.

- **skip**

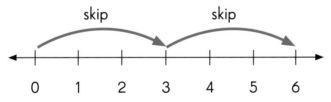

  2 skips of 3 show 2 groups of 3.

- **standard form**

  2,478 is the standard form of two thousand four hundred seventy-eight.

- **sum**

  The sum is the answer to an addition problem.
  123 + 45 = 168
  168 is the sum of 123 and 45.

T

- **ten thousand**

  1 more than 9,999 is 10,000.

- **twice**

  two times

U

- **unit square**

  A unit square is a square with an area of one square unit.

  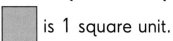 is 1 square unit.

V

- **value**

  In 2,475,
  the value of the digit 2 is 2,000.
  the value of the digit 4 is 400.
  the value of the digit 7 is 70.
  the value of the digit 5 is 5.

W

- **word form**

  Two thousand, four hundred seventy-eight is the word form of 2,478.

Index

Pages listed in black type refer to Pupil Book A.
Pages in blue type refer to Pupil Book B.
Pages in *black italic* type refer to Workbook (WB) A pages.
Pages in *blue italic* type refer to Workbook (WB) B pages.
Pages in **boldface** type show where a term is introduced.

C

D

Pages listed in black type refer to Pupil Book A.
Pages in blue type refer to Pupil Book B.
Pages in *black italic* type refer to Workbook (WB) A pages.
Pages in *blue italic* type refer to Workbook (WB) B pages.
Pages in **boldface** type show where a term is introduced.

Pages listed in black type refer to Pupil Book A.
Pages in blue type refer to Pupil Book B.
Pages in *black italic* type refer to Workbook (WB) A pages.
Pages in *blue italic* type refer to Workbook (WB) B pages.
Pages in **boldface** type show where a term is introduced.

Pages listed in black type refer to Pupil Book A.
Pages in blue type refer to Pupil Book B.
Pages in *black italic* type refer to Workbook (WB) A pages.
Pages in *blue italic* type refer to Workbook (WB) B pages.
Pages in **boldface** type show where a term is introduced.

Mental math
    addition, 37, 41–44, 49–52, 72; *WB 19–20, 25–26, 35*
    division, 216–218; *WB 147–148*
    multiplication, 191–193; *WB 119–120, 152*
    subtraction, 38, 45–48, 72–73; *WB 21–24, 35*
    use to assess reasonableness in solving problems, 38, 40,
        61, 63, 66–69, 71, 73
Meter, 31–32, **35**–41, 63–66, 68, 69–70, 74, 76–78;
    WB 23–30, 41, 46–47, 49
Metric units. *See* Measurement
Mid–Year Review, *WB 187–200*
Mile, 186–**187**,189, 214, 216, 220; *WB 126*
Milliliter, 48–58, 68, 73, 75, 78; *WB 35–39, 43–44, 46,
    48, 50, 254*
Minute, 222, **225**, 226–242, 262, 265; *WB 147–158,
    173, 175*
Missing factor,
    as an unknown, 137, 139–141, 143–145, 147–150,
        159, 184–185, 188–189, 196, 198, 201, 205,
        210, 245, 250; *WB 95–96, 97–98, 100, 102,
        105–106, 109–110, 112–115, 121, 127–134,
        139, 147*
Model equivalent fractions, 121, 122–129, 131, 157, 161
    number line, 124–125, 131, 157
    objects, 122, 138
    pictorial models, 123, 126–129, 131, 157, 161
    strip diagrams, 121, 124, 127
    Model fractions, 114, 116, 130–134, 136–144, 147,
        158–159
    number line, 115–116, 130–132, 140–143, 145, 147
    objects, 117, 120, 138, 149–150, 152–154
    pictorial models, 113, 115, 117–120, 131–132,
        134–140, 144–145, 152–154, 156
    strip diagrams, 113–114, 116, 121, 124, 127, 146
Model numbers to 100,000
    using numbers, 2–35
    using objects, 5–12, 14, 17, 20–23,
    using pictures, 2–3, 13–19, 25, 27–29, 33
Modeling, *See also* Number Line
    addition with fractions, 113, 115; *WB 91, 107–108, 111*
    area, *See* Area – modeling
    congruent figures, *See* Congruent figures
    equivalent fractions, *See* Equivalent Fractions
    fraction circles, *See* Fraction pieces
    line of symmetry, *See* Symmetry – line of
    perimeter, 374–389, 392, 394–397; *WB 223–239,
        247, 250*
    transformations, *See* Geometry – transformations
Models, *See also* Addition; Algebra, Bar Models, Comparisons,
    Division, Drawings, Fractions, Multiplication, Numbers;
    Pictorial models; and Subtraction
    abstract, *throughout. See for example,* 24–25, 29, 69,
        88–89, 114, 125
    bar models, *See* Bar models
    concrete, *throughout. See for example,* 5–12, 14, 17,
        20–23, 117, 120, 122, 138, 149–150, 152–154
    drawings, *See* Drawings
    equations, *throughout. See for example,* 58–62, 65–69,
        72–73, 91, 111, 113, 116, 121, 123–124, 126,
        131, 137, 230, 239, 263, 241–245, 247–248,
        253–255, 257–262, 24–25, 27–30, 63–78,

        230–232, 235–236, 238–245; *WB 30, 34, 36, 38,
        53–54, 68, 80, 82–87, 88, 100, 108, 125–126,
        136, 163–166, 168, 172, 175–176, 178–180;
        WB 41–52*
    manipulatives, *See* Manipulatives
    pictorial, *throughout. See for example,* 2–3, 13–19, 25,
        27–29, 33, 77, 79, 84–86, 94, 98–100, 102–105,
        80–111, 113–121, 123–140, 178–179, 183, 186,
        222–223, 235–236, 281–284, 288–291
    problem–solving models, 41–42, 45–45, 49–50, 53–56,
        58–63, 69–71, 75, 77, 79, 84–86, 90, 93–95,
        98–100, 102–105, 108–110, 115, 118–120, 122,
        126, 127, 128–131, 133–137, 138–149,
        151–155, 157, 158–162, 163–167, 168–175,
        177, 182–183, 185–186, 189, 191–193,
        194–198, 199–209, 210–213, 216–223,
        227–230, 231–234, 235–239, 243–245,
        246–252, 256–262, 264–265, 265–267, 4–10,
        15–19, 21–23, 24–29, 63–77, 346, 349–250,
        356–365, 375–377, 380–383, 390–392
    real objects, *See* Manipulatives
Money
    adding, 4–14; *WB 1–6, 262*
    changing dollars and cents, 2, 3, 11, 20
    counting, 2
    estimating sums, *WB 60*
    making change, *WB 12*
    and place value, 11–12, 20–22
    real–world problems, 24–26; *WB 13–18*
    subtracting, 15–23; *WB 7–12, 262*
    symbols, 1–30; *WB 1–22, 262*
    using, 1–30; *WB 1–22*
    value of a collection of coins and bills, 2, 4–5, 12,
        15–16, 21
Multiple, *See* Skip Counting
Multiplication
    models, 158–161, 164–165, 170–172; *WB 103,
        107, 111*
    arrays, 151–155; *WB 97*
    and division are related, 135–137, 176–181, 183,
        216–219, 223, 237–238; *WB 147–150*
    dot paper arrays, 134, 137, 141–142
    double strategy, 246, 266
    equal groups in, 189, 191, 212, 134, 137, 141–144,
        150–154, 160, 163, 165, 168–172; *WB 121*
    equations, 138–180, 191–209; *WB 93–115, 121–137*
    inverse operation of, *See* Inverse operations
    model using drawings and equations, 152, 158–159,
        163–165, 168, 172, 177, 179–181, 183, 186,
        211, 241–252
    patterns, 160–162, 163–165, 170–171, 181, 188–189,
        191–193, 210
    properties
        Associative, 145, 146–148; *WB 98, 141–142, 193*
        Commutative, 141–144, *WB 96–97, 141*
        Distributive, 134, 137, 141, 143–144, 150, 160,
            163–165, 170–172, 378–379, 381–383
        Identity (*See* Multiplicative Property of One), 138,
            142–144 182
        Multiplicative Property of One, 142–143; *WB 97–98,
            141*

Pages listed in black type refer to Pupil Book A.
Pages in blue type refer to Pupil Book B.
Pages in *black italic* type refer to Workbook (WB) A pages.
Pages in *blue italic* type refer to Workbook (WB) B pages.
Pages in **boldface** type show where a term is introduced.

Pages listed in black type refer to Pupil Book A.
Pages in blue type refer to Pupil Book B.
Pages in *black italic* type refer to Workbook (WB) A pages.
Pages in *blue italic* type refer to Workbook (WB) B pages.
Pages in **boldface** type show where a term is introduced.

is less than (<), *See* Less than symbol
    for unknown numbers in equations, 256, 259–260, 265,
      267
Symmetry, line, *See* Line of Symmetry

Table, *See also* Tally chart
    using data; from, 88, 97–98, 100–101, 104, 106–109;
      WB 80, 83–86, 89–90, 144
Tally chart
    making, 83, 89, 99, 102–103; *WB 62, 65, 78*
    using, 81, 83, 87, 89, 97–99, 102–103; *WB 62–63,*
      65, 78, 137
Tally mark, 81, 83, 87, 89, 97–99, 102–103; *WB 62–63,*
    65, 78, 137
Temperature
    benchmarks 250–252, 256, 263, 265; *WB 159–162,*
      168
    estimation 250–252, 256, 263, 265; *WB 159–161,*
      168, 241
    Fahrenheit temperature, 250–252, 256–257, 259, 261,
      263, 264–265; *WB 159–162, 168, 172, 241*
    real–world problems 256–257, 259, 265; *WB 168, 172*
Tens, *See* Place value
Thermometer, 250–252, 263, 265; *WB 163–166*
Thinking skills
    analyzing parts and whole, 89, 114, 263; *WB 18, 38,*
      72, 87–88, 118, 139–140, 157–158, 179–180;
      WB 22, 40, 175–176, 241
    classifying, 127, 56; *WB 55; WB 89–90, 214*
    comparing, 69, 27, 56, 105, 156, 261, 390; *WB 17,*
      69–70, 117; WB 21, 87–88, 117–118, 136,
      175–176, 213–214, 239, 242
    deduction, 32, 56, 105, 213, 261; *WB 37, 57; WB 22,*
      87–88, 136, 241
    identifying patterns and relationships, 89, 114, 181, 210,
      235, 105, 261, 390; *WB 58, 71, 186; WB 27,*
      87–88, 214, 240, 242
    making inferences, 127, 105; *WB 87–88*
    real–world problems, 127, 265; *WB 38, 71–72,*
      179–180
    sequencing, *WB 117–118*
    spatial visualization, 75, 156, 294–295, 339;
      WB 51–52, 135, 195–198, 213–214, 239
Thousands, *See* Place value
Time
    add and subtract time intervals, 239–249, 255,
      257–258, 260–262, 264–265;
    a.m. and p.m., *See also* a.m. and p.m.
    before and after the hour, 222, 224, 226–227, 244,
      249, 265
    intervals, *See* Elapsed time
    telling
        to the hour, half–hour, quarter–hour, 222, 224,
          226–227, 229; *WB 147*
        to the minute, 225–229, 262, 264; *WB 147–150*
    units of, 220
Time line, 243–248, 255, 262; *WB 157, 170, 263*
Total number, interpret products of numbers as, *See* Product

Transformations, *See* Geometry
Turns, **323**, 324, 329–330, 340, 344; *WB 207, 210,*
    213–214, 246
Two–dimensional figures, *See* Plane figures.

Unit fraction,
    explain as a part of a whole, 113–115, 117, 157
    on a number line, 124, 131, 140–143, 145, 147, 157,
      159
    use to partition fraction models, 113–115–118, 121
Unknown factor, division as, *See* Division –as an unknown
    factor problem
Unknowns in equations, determine, *throughout. See for*
    example, 37–42, 44–46, 48–50, 52, 61–63, 70–73,
      122–123, 238, 242–250, 253–254, 256–259, 3–12,
      14–21, 23–25, 27–30, 69–73, 254–255
Unknowns,
    in addition and subtraction word problems, 86–87, 91,
      111, 113, 116,122–131; 24–26, 63–66, 68–74,
      76–78; *WB 53–54,68, 71–78; WB 13–22, 41–52,*
      262
    letters for, in equations, 256, 259–260, 265, 267
    in multiplication and division word problems, 245–265,
      60, 62, 66–69, 71–74, 76–78; *WB 167–186,*
      198–199; WB 41–42, 44–48, 262
Unlike fractions, *See* Fractions, unlike
    comparing, 137–144, 146–148, 158–159, 162;
      WB 101–106, 138–139
    ordering,142–143, 145–147,158–159,161; *WB 106,139*

Value, 12
    of a collection of coins and bills, *See* Money
Vertex (vertices) of a plane figure, 307–**308**, 317, 340–341;
    WB 199–202, 204
Visual thinking. *See also* Graphs; Math reasoning; Problem
    Solving
Volume, **50**, 66, 73, 76; *WB 35–38, 254*
Vocabulary, *throughout. See for example,* 5, 12, 20, 35, 53,
    64, 72, 77, 79, 91, 94, 98, 116, 122, 130, 138, 151,
    158, 176, 184, 194, 212, 219, 224, 238, 243, 246,
    35, 38, 42, 48, 58, 84, 97, 108, 117, 121, 126, 130,
    160, 168, 186, 202, 214, 223, 228, 241, 248, 262,
    266, 275, 279, 285, 296, 303, 320, 330, 340, 347,
    353, 362, 371, 384

Weight
    benchmarks, 190–203, 218; *WB 127–128, 130, 142*
    estimation 190–203, 214, 217–218; *WB 127–130,
        142*
    non–standard units, 190–193, 195, 197, 201–203;
        WB 127–128, 142
Whole numbers
    comparing, 20–34; *WB 11–16*
    as fractions, *See* Fractions – whole numbers as,
    interpret products and quotients of, 133–134, 157,
        158–159, 162, 167, 176–177, 178–179, 183,
        214–215, 219
    ordering, 20–34; *WB 11–16*
    place value, 12–19, 24–26, 30–34; *WB 5–11, 17–18*
Word form, 5–6, 10, 13, 15, 19, 33–34; *WB 2–3, 7–8*
    for inequality symbols, 114, 116, 131–132, 124, 140,
        145, 158–159, 162, 196, 203; *WB 103–105, 117,
        139, 142*
    time, 222, 225–229, 264; *WB 143–146*
    Word problems. *See* Real–world problems

Yard, 183–185, 189, 212, 214, 217–218; *WB 120–122*

Zero
    in multiplication, *See* Multiplication
    subtracting across, *See* Subtraction
Zero Property of multiplication, *See* Multiplication and
    Properties of numbers.

Photo Credits

Cover: ©Houghton Mifflin Harcourt, *xi*: ©Marshall Cavendish Education, *1tl*: ©INMAGINE.com, *1tr*: ©STOCKCONNECTION/INMAGINE.com, *1bl*: ©INMAGINE.com, *1br*: ©INMAGINE.com, *5bl*: ©Stockbyte Photo CD, *5br*: ©Stockbyte Photo CD, *7*: ©JupiterImages Photo CD, *12*: ©Stockbyte Photo CD, *13*: ©iStockphoto.com/Sean Locke, *17*: ©iStockphoto.com/quavondo; *20*: ©Stockbyte Photo CD, *24t*: ©iStockphoto.com/JBryson, *24m*: ©Image Source Photo CD, *37*: ©iStockphoto.com, *42*: ©iStockphoto.com/Bob Thomas, *46*: ©Stockbyte Photo CD, *49*: ©iStockphoto.com/Reuben Schulz, *50t*: ©Stockbyte Photo CD, *50b*: ©Image Source Photo CD, *55*: ©Image Source Photo CD, *58t*: ©Stockbyte Photo CD, *58m*: ©Image Source Photo CD, *59t*: ©iStockphoto.com/Sean Locke, *59m*: ©JupiterImages Photo CD, *59b*: ©Image Source Photo CD, *61*: ©iStockphoto.com/Drew Meredith, *62*: ©Stockbyte Photo CD, *65t*: ©iStockphoto.com/Sean Locke, *65m*: ©Image Source Photo CD, *66t*: ©Stockbyte Photo CD, *66m*: ©iStockphoto.com, *89*: ©iStockphoto.com/Drew Meredith, *95*: ©Stockbyte Photo CD, *97*: ©Image Source Photo CD, *99*: ©Image Source Photo CD, *101*: ©iStockphoto.com/Reuben Schulz, *102*: ©iStockphoto.com/Bob Thomas, *103*: ©iStockphoto.com/JBryson, *104*: ©Image Source Photo CD, *106*: ©Stockbyte Photo CD, *108m*: ©Stockbyte Photo CD, *108b*: ©Image Source Photo CD, *109*: ©JupiterImages Photo CD, *110*: ©iStockphoto.com/Reuben Schulz, *111*: ©Image Source Photo CD, *122*: ©iStockphoto.com/Drew Meredith, *123*: ©iStockphoto.com/Jaroslaw Wojcik, *124t*: ©iStockphoto.com/Sean Locke, *124m*: ©Stockbyte Photo CD, *124b*: ©JupiterImages Photo CD, *125tl*: ©Image Source Photo CD, *125ml*: ©Image Source Photo CD, *125bl*: ©Image Source Photo CD, *125tr*: ©iStockphoto.com/Annett Vauteck, *125mr*: ©iStockphoto.com/Annett Vauteck, *125br*: ©iStockphoto.com/Annett Vauteck, *138m*: ©iStockphoto.com/Annett Vauteck, *138b*: ©iStockphoto.com/OGphoto, *142*: ©iStockphoto.com/Jani Bryson, *144*: ©Image Source Photo CD, *151m*: ©iStockphoto.com/Drew Meredith, *151b*: ©Stockbyte Photo CD, *153*: ©Image Source Photo CD, *154*: ©iStockphoto.com/Jacek Chabraszewski, *158m*: ©iStockphoto.com/Jaroslaw Wojcik, *158b*: ©JupiterImages Photo CD, *160*: ©Image Source Photo CD, *163m*: ©iStockphoto.com/Nina Shannon, *163b*: ©iStockphoto.com/Annett Vauteck, *164*: ©iStockphoto.com/Linda Kloosterhof, *165*: ©Image Source Photo CD, *168m*: ©Stockbyte Photo CD, *168b*: ©iStockphoto.com/Bob Thomas, *170t*: ©iStockphoto.com/Sean Locke, *170b*: ©Image Source Photo CD, *173*: ©iStockphoto.com/JBryson, *176*: ©Marshall Cavendish Education, *176*: ©Image Source Photo CD, *177*: ©Stockbyte Photo CD, *178*: ©Marshall Cavendish Education, *178*: ©Stockbyte Photo CD, *179*: ©iStockphoto.com/Sean Locke, *181*: ©iStockphoto.com/Jaroslaw Wojcik, *187t*: ©Marshall Cavendish Education, *187bl*: ©iStockphoto.com/Annett Vauteck, *187br*: ©iStockphoto.com/Jaroslaw Wojcik, *191*: ©iStockphoto.com/Nina Shannon, *192t*: ©Stockbyte Photo CD, *192b*: ©iStockphoto.com, *193*: ©Image Source Photo CD, *198t*: ©iStockphoto.com/Pathathai Chungyam, *198m*: ©iStockphoto.com/Jani Bryson, *210*: ©JupiterImages Photo CD, *216t*: ©Stockbyte Photo CD, *216m*: ©iStockphoto.com/Drew Meredith, *216b*: ©Stockbyte Photo CD, *217t*: ©iStockphoto.com/Pathathai Chungyam, *217b*: ©iStockphoto.com/quavondo, *219*: ©iStockphoto.com/Reuben Schulz, *220m*: ©Marshall Cavendish Education, *220m*: ©Image Source Photo CD, *220b*: ©iStockphoto.com/Annett Vauteck, *221t*: ©Marshall Cavendish Education, *221m*: ©iStockphoto.com/Jacek Chabraszewski, *223*: ©iStockphoto.com/Sean Locke, *224*: ©Marshall Cavendish Education, *225t*: ©Image Source Photo CD, *225b*: ©JupiterImages Photo CD, *233*: ©iStockphoto.com/Reuben Schulz, *244*: ©iStockphoto.com/Reuben Schulz, *245*: ©iStockphoto.com/daaronj, *246*: ©iStockphoto.com, *247*: ©Stockbyte Photo CD, *257*: ©iStockphoto.com/Reuben Schulz, *263*: ©JupiterImages Photo CD, *271*: ©Marshall Cavendish Education, *276*: ©Marshall Cavendish Education

COMMON CORE STATE STANDARDS FOR MATHEMATICAL CONTENT

STANDARD	DESCRIPTOR	PAGE CITATIONS
3.OA OPERATIONS AND ALGEBRAIC THINKING		
Represent and solve problems involving multiplication and division.		
3.OA.1	Interpret products of whole numbers, e.g., interpret 5 × 7 as the total number of objects in 5 groups of 7 objects each.	SE 3A: 132–137, 151–157, 158–162, 163–167
3.OA.2	Interpret whole-number quotients of whole numbers, e.g., interpret 56 ÷ 8 as the number of objects in each share when 56 objects are partitioned equally into 8 shares, or as a number of shares when 56 objects are partitioned into equal shares of 8 objects each.	SE 3A: 132–137, 176–177, 178–180, 214–215
3.OA.3	Use multiplication and division within 100 to solve word problems in situations involving equal groups, arrays, and measurement quantities, e.g., by using drawings and equations with a symbol for the unknown number to represent the problem.	SE 3A: 151–157, 158–162, 163–167, 168–175, 176–177, 178–180, 219–223, 227–230, 231–234, 240–242, 243–245, 246–252, 253–255, 256–262 SE 3B: 59–62, 63–68, 69–74
3.OA.4	Determine the unknown whole number in a multiplication or division equation relating three whole numbers.	SE 3A: 138–150, 151–157, 158–162, 163–167, 168–175, 176–177, 178–180, 191–193, 194–198, 199–209, 216–218, 219–223, 224–226, 227–230, 231–234, 243–245, 246–252, 253–255, 256–262 SE 3B: 59–62, 63–68, 69–74
Understand properties of multiplication and the relationship between multiplication and division.		
3.OA.5	Apply properties of operations as strategies to multiply and divide.	SE 3A: 138–150, 151–157, 158–162, 163–167, 168–175, 176–177, 178–180, 191–193, 194–198, 199–209, 216–218, 219–223, 224–226, 227–230, 231–234, 243–245, 246–252, 253–255, 256–262 SE 3B: 63–68, 69–74
3.OA.6	Understand division as an unknown-factor problem.	SE 3A: 132–137, 176–177, 178–180, 216–218, 219–223, 224–226, 227–230, 231–234, 253–255, 256–263 SE 3B: 63–68, 69–74

COMMON CORE STATE STANDARDS FOR MATHEMATICAL CONTENT

STANDARD	DESCRIPTOR	PAGE CITATIONS
Multiply and divide within 100.		
3.OA.7	Fluently multiply and divide within 100, using strategies such as the relationship between multiplication and division (e.g., knowing that 8 × 5 = 40, one knows 40 ÷ 5 = 8) or properties of operations. By the end of Grade 3, know from memory all products of two one-digit numbers.	SE 3A: 138–150, 151–157, 158–162, 163–167, 176–177, 178–180, 191–193, 194–198, 199–209, 216–218, 219–223, 224–226, 227–230, 231–234, 243–245, 246–252, 253–255, 256–262 SE 3B: 63–68, 69–74
Solve problems involving the four operations, and identify and explain patterns in arithmetic.		
3.OA.8	Solve two-step word problems using the four operations. Represent these problems using equations with a letter standing for the unknown quantity. Assess the reasonableness of answers using mental computation and estimation strategies including rounding.	SE 3A: 53–63, 117–121, 122–126, 127, 132–137,181, 246–252, 256–262, 263
3.OA.9	Identify arithmetic patterns (including patterns in the addition table or multiplication table) and explain them using properties of operations.	SE 3A: 5–11, 20–31, 89, 151–157, 158–162, 163–167, 168–175, 191–193, 219–223, 224–226
3.NBT NUMBER AND OPERATIONS IN BASE TEN		
Use place value understanding and properties of operations to perform multi-digit arithmetic.		
3.NBT.1	Use place value understanding to round whole numbers to the nearest 10 or 100.	SE 3A: 36–40, 53–63, 69
3.NBT.2	Fluently add and subtract within 1000 using strategies and algorithms based on place value, properties of operations, and/or the relationship between addition and subtraction.	SE 3A: 41–44, 45–48, 49–52, 53–63, 64–69, 74–76, 77–78, 79–83, 84–87, 89, 92–93, 94–97, 98–101, 102–107, 108–113, 114, 122–126 SE 3B: 4–14, 15–23, 24–26, 63–68, 69–74, 374–383
3.NBT.3	Multiply one-digit whole numbers by multiples of 10 in the range 10–90 (e.g., 9 × 80, 5 × 60) using strategies based on place value and properties of operations.	SE 3A: 32, 151–157, 158–162, 163–167, 168–175, 191–193, 199–209

COMMON CORE STATE STANDARDS FOR MATHEMATICAL CONTENT

STANDARD	DESCRIPTOR	PAGE CITATIONS
3.NF NUMBER AND OPERATIONS - FRACTIONS		
Develop understanding of fractions as numbers.		
3.NF.1	Understand a fraction 1/b as the quantity formed by 1 part when a whole is partitioned into b equal parts; understand a fraction a/b as the quantity formed by a parts of size 1/b.	SE 3B: 112–116, 121–125, 126–129, 149–155, 163–167
3.NF.2	Understand a fraction as a number on the number line; represent fractions on a number line diagram.	
3.NF.2.a	Represent a fraction 1/b on a number line diagram by defining the interval from 0 to 1 as the whole and partitioning it into b equal parts. Recognize that each part has size 1/b and that the endpoint of the part based at 0 locates the number 1/b on the number line.	SE 3B: 117–120, 121–125, 130–148
3.NF.2.b	Represent a fraction a/b on a number line diagram by marking off a lengths 1/b from 0. Recognize that the resulting interval has size a/b and that its endpoint locates the number a/b on the number line.	SE 3B: 121–125, 130–148, 163–167
3.NF.3	Explain equivalence of fractions in special cases, and compare fractions by reasoning about their size.	
3.NF.3.a	Understand two fractions as equivalent (equal) if they are the same size, or the same point on a number line.	SE 3B: 121–125, 126–129, 130–148
3.NF.3.b	Recognize and generate simple equivalent fractions, (e.g., 1/2 = 2/4, 4/6 = 2/3). Explain why the fractions are equivalent, e.g., by using a visual fraction model.	SE 3B: 121–125, 126–129, 130–148
3.NF.3.c	Express whole numbers as fractions and recognize fractions that are equivalent to whole numbers.	SE 3B: 112–116, 117–120, 149–155
3.NF.3.d	Compare two fractions with the same numerator or the same denominator by reasoning about their size. Recognize that comparisons are valid only when the two fractions refer to the same whole. Record the results of comparisons with the symbols >, =, or <, and justify the conclusions, e.g., by using a visual fraction model.	SE 3B: 112–116, 130–148

STANDARD	DESCRIPTOR	PAGE CITATIONS
3.MD MEASUREMENT AND DATA		
Solve problems involving measurement and estimation of intervals of time, liquid volumes, and masses of objects.		
3.MD.1	Tell and write time to the nearest minute and measure time intervals in minutes. Solve word problems involving addition and subtraction of time intervals in minutes, e.g., by representing the problem on a number line diagram.	SE 3B: 221–224, 225–229, 230–234, 235–238, 239–242, 243–249, 253–260
3.MD.2	Measure and estimate liquid volumes and masses of objects using standard units of grams (g), kilograms (kg), and liters (L). Add, subtract, multiply, or divide to solve one-step word problems involving masses or volumes that are given in the same units, e.g., by using drawings (such as a beaker with a measurement scale) to represent the problem.	SE 3B: 31–34, 42–47, 48–55, 63–68, 69–74
Represent and interpret data.		
3.MD.3	Draw a scaled picture graph and a scaled bar graph to represent a data set with several categories. Solve one- and two-step "how many more" and "how many less" problems using information presented in scaled bar graphs.	SE 3B: 84–90, 91–96, 97–104
3.MD.4	Generate measurement data by measuring lengths using rulers marked with halves and fourths of an inch. Show the data by making a line plot, where the horizontal scale is marked off in appropriate units—whole numbers, halves, or quarters.	SE 3B: 97–104, 168–189
3.MD.5	Recognize area as an attribute of plane figures and understand concepts of area measurement.	
3.MD.5.a	A square with side length 1 unit, called "a unit square," is said to have "one square unit" of area, and can be used to measure area.	SE 3B: 349–355, 356–364, 365–373, 374–383
3.MD.5.b	A plane figure which can be covered without gaps or overlaps by *n* unit squares is said to have an area of *n* square units.	SE 3B: 349–355, 356–364, 365–373, 374–383
3.MD.6	Measure areas by counting unit squares (square centimeters, square meters, square inches, square feet, and improvised units).	SE 3B: 349–355, 356–364, 365–373, 374–383

COMMON CORE STATE STANDARDS FOR MATHEMATICAL CONTENT

STANDARD	DESCRIPTOR	PAGE CITATIONS
3.MD.7	Relate area to the operations of multiplication and addition.	
3.MD.7.a	Find the area of a rectangle with whole-number side lengths by tiling it, and show that the area is the same as would be found by multiplying the side lengths.	SE 3B: 345–348, 349–355, 374–383
3.MD.7.b	Multiply side lengths to find areas of rectangles with whole-number side lengths in the context of solving real world and mathematical problems, and represent whole-number products as rectangular areas in mathematical reasoning.	SE 3B: 365–373, 374–383
3.MD.7.c	Use tiling to show in a concrete case that the area of a rectangle with whole-number side lengths a and $b + c$ is the sum of $a \times b$ and $a \times c$. Use area models to represent the distributive property in mathematical reasoning.	SE 3A: 158–162, 163–167, 168–175 SE 3B: 345–348
3.MD.7.d	Recognize area as additive. Find areas of rectilinear figures by decomposing them into non-overlapping rectangles and adding the areas of the non-overlapping parts, applying this technique to solve real world problems.	SE 3A: 158–162, 163–167, 168–175 SE 3B: 356–364, 365–373, 374–383

Geometric measurement: recognize perimeter as an attribute of plane figures and distinguish between linear and area measures.

STANDARD	DESCRIPTOR	PAGE CITATIONS
3.MD.8	Solve real world and mathematical problems involving perimeters of polygons, including finding the perimeter given the side lengths, finding an unknown side length, and exhibiting rectangles with the same perimeter and different areas, or with the same area and different perimeters.	SE 3B: 374–383, 384–389

3.G GEOMETRY

Reason with shapes and their attributes.

STANDARD	DESCRIPTOR	PAGE CITATIONS
3.G.1	Understand that shapes in different categories (e.g., rhombuses, rectangles, and others) may share attributes (e.g., having four sides), and that the shared attributes can define a larger category (e.g., quadrilaterals). Recognize rhombuses, rectangles, and squares as examples of quadrilaterals, and draw examples of quadrilaterals that do not belong to any of these subcategories.	SE 3B: 268–276, 277–280, 305–320, 332–338
3.G.2	Partition shapes into parts with equal areas. Express the area of each part as a unit fraction of the whole.	SE 3B: 117–120, 121–125, 126–129, 149–155

COMMON CORE STATE STANDARDS FOR MATHEMATICAL PRACTICE

STANDARDS	PAGE CITATIONS

1. MAKE SENSE OF PROBLEMS AND PERSEVERE IN SOLVING THEM.

How *Math in Focus*® Aligns:

Math in Focus® is built around the Singapore Ministry of Education's mathematics framework pentagon, which places mathematical problem solving at the core of the curriculum. Encircling the pentagon are the skills and knowledge needed to develop successful problem solvers, with concepts, skills, and processes building a foundation for attitudes and metacognition. *Math in Focus*® is based on the premise that, in order for students to persevere and solve both routine and non-routine problems, they need to be given tools that they can use consistently and successfully. They need to understand both the how and the why of math so that they can self-monitor and become empowered problem solvers. This in turn spurs positive attitudes that allow students to solidify their learning and enjoy mathematics. *Math in Focus*® teaches content through a problem solving perspective. Strong emphasis is placed on the concrete-pictorial-abstract progression to solve and master problems. This leads to strong conceptual understanding. Problem solving is embedded throughout the program.

SE 3A: 5–11, 20–31, 32, 41–44, 45–48, 49–52, 53–63, 64–68, 69, 79–83, 84–87, 89, 92–93, 94–97, 98–101, 102–107, 108–113, 114, 122–126, 127, 138–150, 151–157, 158–162, 163–167, 168–175, 181, 191–193, 219–223, 224–226, 246–252, 253–255, 256–262, 263

SE 3B: 24–26, 69–74, 75, 84–90, 91–96, 97–104, 149–155, 204–212, 213, 225–229, 261, 287–293, 294–295, 332–338, 339, 384–389, 390

2. REASON ABSTRACTLY AND QUANTITATIVELY.

How *Math in Focus*® Aligns:

Math in Focus® concrete-pictorial-abstract progression helps students effectively contextualize and decontextualize situations by developing a deep mastery of concepts. Each topic is approached with the expectation that students will understand both how it works, and also why. Students start by experiencing the concept through hands-on manipulative use. Then, they must translate what they learned in the concrete stage into a visual representation of the concept. Finally, once they have gained a strong understanding, they are able to represent the concept abstractly. Once students reach the abstract stage, they have had enough exposure to the concept and they are able to manipulate it and apply it in multiple contexts. They are also able to extend and make inferences; this prepares them for success in more advanced levels of mathematics. They are able to both use the symbols and also understand why they work, which allows students to relate them to other situations and apply them effectively.

SE 3A: 20–31, 32, 64–68, 69, 84–87, 89, 114, 122–126, 127, 151–157, 178–180, 181, 199–209, 216–218, 219–223, 231–234, 256–262, 263

SE 3B: 15–23, 38–41, 56, 69–74, 97–104, 204–212, 213, 225–229, 243–249, 253–260, 287–293, 332–338, 339, 384–389

3. CONSTRUCT VIABLE ARGUMENTS AND CRITIQUE THE REASONING OF OTHERS.

How *Math in Focus*® Aligns:

As seen on the Singapore Mathematics Framework pentagon, metacognition is a foundational part of the Singapore curriculum. Students are taught to self-monitor, so they can determine whether or not their solutions make sense. Journal questions and other opportunities to explain their thinking are found throughout the program. Students are systematically taught to use visual diagrams to represent mathematical relationships in such a way as to not only accurately solve problems, but also to justify their answers. Chapters conclude with a Put On Your Thinking Cap! problem. This is a comprehensive opportunity for students to apply concepts and present viable arguments. Games, explorations, and hands-on activities are also strategically placed in chapters when students are learning concepts. During these collaborative experiences, students interact with one another to construct viable arguments and critique the reasoning of others in a constructive manner. In addition, thought bubbles provide tutorial guidance throughout the entire Student Book. These scaffolded dialogues help students articulate concepts, check for understanding, analyze, justify conclusions, and self-regulate if necessary.

SE 3A: 20–31, 79–83, 125, 138–150, 181

SE 3B: 91–96, 130–148, 149–155, 213, 268–276, 305–320, 339, 349–355, 365–373, 374–383

COMMON CORE STATE STANDARDS FOR MATHEMATICAL PRACTICE

STANDARDS	PAGE CITATIONS

4. MODEL WITH MATHEMATICS.

How *Math in Focus*® Aligns:

Math in Focus® follows a concrete-pictorial-abstract progression, introducing concepts first with physical manipulatives or objects, then moving to pictorial representation, and finally on to abstract symbols. A number of models are found throughout the program that support the pictorial stage of learning.

Math in Focus® places a strong emphasis on number and number relationships, using place-value manipulatives and place-value charts to model concepts consistently throughout the program. In all grades, operations are modeled with place-value materials so students understand how the standard algorithms work. Even the mental math instruction uses understanding of place value to model how mental arithmetic can be understood and done. These place-value models build throughout the program to cover increasingly complex concepts. Singapore Math® is also known for its use of model drawing, often called "bar modeling" in the U.S. Model drawing is a systematic method of representing word problems and number relationships that is explicitly taught beginning in Grade 2 and extends all the way to secondary school. Students are taught to use rectangular "bars" to represent the relationship between known and unknown numerical quantities and to solve problems related to these quantities. This gives students the tools to develop mastery and tackle problems as they become increasingly more complex.

SE 3A: 5–11, 12–19, 53–63, 77–78, 79–83, 84–87, 92–93, 94–97, 98–101, 102–107, 108–113, 114, 122–126, 127, 138–150, 151–157, 158–162, 163–167, 168–175, 176–177, 178–180, 194–198, 199–209, 224–226, 227–230, 231–234, 243–245, 246–252, 253_255, 256–262, 263

SE 3B: 4–14, 15–23, 24–26, 42–47, 48–55, 63–68, 69–74, 105, 117–120, 121–125, 126–129, 130–148, 149–155, 168–189, 190–203, 204–212, 213, 225–229, 243–249, 250–252, 253–260, 261, 294–295, 365–373

5. USE APPROPRIATE TOOLS STRATEGICALLY.

How *Math in Focus*® Aligns:

Math in Focus® helps students explore the different mathematical tools that are available to them. New concepts are introduced using concrete objects, which help students break down concepts to develop mastery. They learn how to use these manipulatives to attain a better understanding of the problem and solve it appropriately. *Math in Focus*® includes representative pictures and icons as well as thought bubbles that model the thought processes students should use with the tools. Several examples are listed below. Additional tools referenced and used in the program include clocks, money, dot paper, place-value charts, geometric tools, and figures.

SE 3A: 5–11, 12–19, 41–44, 45–48, 49–52, 53–63, 77–78, 79–83, 84–87, 92–93, 94–97, 98–101, 102–107, 108–113, 114, 138–150, 151–157, 163–167, 168–175, 194–198, 199–209, 219–223, 227–230, 231–234

SE 3B: 4–14, 42–47, 56, 63–68, 84–90, 91–96, 97–104, 121–125, 130–148, 168–189, 190–203, 204–212, 225–229, 261, 268–276, 277–280, 281–286, 287–293, 294–295, 305–320, 322–330, 332–338, 356–364, 365–373, 374–383

6. ATTEND TO PRECISION.

How *Math in Focus*® Aligns:

As seen in the Singapore Mathematics Framework, metacognition, or the ability to monitor one's own thinking, is key in Singapore Math®. This is modeled for students throughout *Math in Focus*® through the use of thought bubbles, journal writing, and prompts to explain reasoning. When students are taught to monitor their own thinking, they are better able to attend to precision, as they consistently ask themselves, "Does this make sense?" This questioning requires students to be able to understand and explain their reasoning to others, as well as catch mistakes early on and identify when incorrect labels or units have been used. Additionally, precise language is an important aspect of *Math in Focus*®. Students attend to the precision of language with terms like factor, quotient, difference, and capacity.

SE 3A: 20–31, 53–63, 64–68, 69, 79–83, 94–97, 122–126, 138–150, 178–180, 194–198

SE 3B: 4–14, 56, 84–90, 91–96, 97–104, 105, 121–125, 130–148, 168–189, 190–203, 204–212, 225–229, 243–249, 261, 268–276, 277–280, 281–286, 287–293, 305–320, 322–330, 332–338, 349–355, 365–373, 356–364, 374–383, 384–389

COMMON CORE STATE STANDARDS FOR MATHEMATICAL PRACTICE

STANDARDS	PAGE CITATIONS
7. LOOK FOR AND MAKE USE OF STRUCTURE.	
How *Math in Focus*® Aligns: The inherent pedagogy of Singapore Math® allows students to look for, and make use of, structure. Place value is one of the underlying principles in ***Math in Focus***®. Concepts in the program start simple and grow in complexity throughout the chapter, year, and grade. This helps students master the structure of a given skill, see its utility, and advance to higher levels. Many of the models in the program, particularly number bonds and bar models, allow students to easily see patterns within concepts and make inferences. As students progress through grade levels, this level of structure becomes more advanced.	SE 3A: 20–31, 32, 114 SE 3B: 75, 130–148, 149–155, 339, 365–373
8. LOOK FOR AND EXPRESS REGULARITY IN REPEATED REASONING.	
How *Math in Focus*® Aligns: A strong foundation in place value, combined with modeling tools such as bar modeling and number bonds, gives students the foundation they need to look for and express regularity in repeated reasoning. Operations are taught with place value materials so students understand how the standard algorithms work in all grades. Even the mental math instruction uses understanding of place value to model how mental arithmetic can be understood and done. This allows students to learn shortcuts for solving problems and understand why they work. Additionally, because students are given consistent tools for solving problems, they have the opportunity to see the similarities in how different problems are solved and understand efficient means for solving them. Throughout the program, students see regularity with the reasoning and patterns between the four key operations. Students continually evaluate the reasonableness of solutions throughout the program; the consistent models for solving, checking, and self-regulation help them validate their answers.	SE 3A: 41–44, 45–48, 49–52, 53–63, 64–68, 79–83, 84–87, 92–93, 94–97, 98–101, 102–107, 108–113, 122–126, 138–150, 151–157, 158–162, 163–167, 168–175, 176–177, 191–193, 194–198, 199–209, 216–218, 219–223, 227–230, 231–234, 243–245, 246–252, 253–255, 256–262 SE 3B: 4–14, 15–23, 24–26, 384–389, 390